Creating the customer-driven car company

to Bob Lutz
customer-driven car company executive
and good friend

Creating the customer-driven car company

Karl E. Ludvigsen
Chairman, Ludvigsen Associates Limited

INTERNATIONAL THOMSON BUSINESS PRESS

I ⓣ P An International Thomson Publishing Company

London • Bonn • Boston • Johannesburg • Madrid • Melbourne • Mexico City • New York • Paris
Singapore • Tokyo • Toronto • Albany, NY • Belmont, CA • Cincinnati, OH • Detroit, MI

Creating the customer-driven car company

Copyright © Karl E. Ludvigsen

First published 1996 by International Thomson Business Press

I(T)P   A division of International Thomson Publishing Inc.
The ITP logo is a trademark under licence

British Library Cataloguing-in-Publication Data
A catalogue record for this book is available from the British Library
Library of Congress Catalog Card Number: 96-68835

First edition 1996

Typeset by Florencetype Ltd, Stoodleigh Court, Devon
Printed in the UK by Clays Ltd, St Ives plc, Bungay, Suffolk

ISBN 0-412-73760-4 (ITBP edition)
ISBN 1-56091-851-9 (SAE edition)

International Thomson Business Press
Berkshire House
168–173 High Holborn
London WC1V 7AA
UK

International Thomson Business Press
20 Park Plaza
13th Floor
Boston MA 02116
USA

http://www.thomson.com/itbp.html

Contents

Foreword

Students of the auto industry are constantly barraged by an ongoing stream of news and facts, stretched out over years, if not decades. It's often difficult to discern a pattern in these developments, much less organize them into a comprehensive explanation of what is going on in the industry, or how auto makers can exploit them. Yet Karl Ludvigsen has achieved this, and more.

With this book, Ludvigsen introduces us to his concept of 'customerizing', that is, how to gear up all areas of a company to focus exclusively on their customers. It's not as if no one has thought of these ideas before. Indeed, Ludvigsen amply (and generously) documents the many sources he uses to construct his analysis. But rather than just string a collection of facts together, he weaves the information into a comprehensive explanation of what it takes to build a customer-driven company. The result is an extremely valuable contribution to the automotive industry.

Karl uses his unique background and experience to explain how companies must customerize. Rather than just bore in on one or two areas, he covers it all, starting with R&D then marching the reader through design, production, sales and service. Moreover, he peppers his narrative with real-world examples from Europe, the USA and Japan and in the process raises some hard questions for auto makers, especially as it pertains to dealers.

People who are not directly involved in building a customer-driven automotive company can still learn a lot from this book. Not only does it contains a wealth of information, it's written in a way that cuts through complex issues very simply. And while the examples Karl uses are taken exclusively from the auto industry, it takes little imagination to see how his customerizing concepts can be applied to virtually any industry. Better still, for those who are not in a managerial position that gives them the authority to revamp an entire company, the lessons provided here can be applied to any department, or process. Rarely does a book provide such comprehensive coverage of the auto industry, with insight and lessons that can be used by such a wide-ranging number of people and disciplines.

I am sure you will enjoy reading this book and will feel rewarded by the insight it conveys.

John McElroy,
Editorial Director, Automotive
Industries, Detroit, Michigan

Introduction

This book is the result of 40 years of study and activity by its author in the world motor business. It relies heavily on research and analysis undertaken by two companies in which I am active: Euromotor Reports Limited, a researcher and publisher of special motor-business studies since 1989, and Ludvigsen Associates Limited, a management consulting and services resource for the world motor industry since 1983.

This activity has led me to the following conclusion: consideration of customer needs as a first priority in every aspect of the auto business is not only possible but essential for future success and profitability. We call it 'customerizing'. And throughout the book I say 'we' rather than 'I' in recognition of the research and analysis contributions made by my colleagues. Many thanks to them all.

Inspiration for this conclusion was provided by my participation in the AutoTrends Panels organized by the advertising agency Ogilvy & Mather. Specific examples cited in the Panel meetings have been referenced in the references. I owe particular thanks to Graham Phillips, Kelly O'Dea and Jan Daniel Starr of Ogilvy & Mather for their support of my participation. Many valuable points and comments were made by other Ogilvy & Mather personnel.

I also owe a debt to those contributors to the studies and reports of Euromotor Reports whose findings provide some of the foundation for the conclusions and recommendations of this study. In particular I wish to mention and recognize Nigel S. Hills and A.T. Lowry, whose reports are referred to in the references. Help in preparing this book for publication has been provided by Dr Darren Hall of Euromotor Reports and Christine Lalla of the Ludvigsen Library.

The work carried out to prepare the original study on which this book is based was underwritten in significant part by the Burda publishing company of Munich, Germany and its weekly magazine, *Bunte*. Particularly involved was Hans-Peter Baron von Thyssen-Bornemisszsa, whose support and interest are gratefully acknowledged.

A preview of this study was presented in April 1993 at the Burda-Auto-Forum, for which it was commissioned. A shorter version was published by Euromotor Reports under the title *Coming out of the Car Crisis – Customers to the Rescue* in both English and German.

A German version of the present text was published in 1995 by the Verlag Moderne Industrie, Landsberg.

I appreciate very much the interest of International Thomson Business Press in this work and its publishing of this version in English. At International Thomson Business Press I am especially indebted to Mark Wellings for his support and encouragement.

By naming those above I am not seeking to evade the responsibility for the contents and the conclusions of the book, which are down to me alone.

This book has been written at a critical period in the evolution of the car business, not only in Europe but throughout the world. I hope it will make some small contribution to the future success of that business. Of course, its findings are also of relevance and importance to vehicle industries in general and indeed to other industries in other regions and nations of the globe.

Now it is time for me to step aside and invite the customer to step forward.

Karl E. Ludvigsen
Islington, London
March 1996

The buyers' market for cars – customers take command

1

Customers have taken over the management of the world's car business. It didn't happen all at once; some car makers are still at war with their customers and don't realize that their colleagues have capitulated.

Among the enlightened suppliers of cars and parts, awareness is increasing that decisions are no longer being taken on 'the fourteenth floor' or along 'mahogany row'. They are being made instead by the end customers who buy and use their products.

USA BECAME BUYERS' MARKET FOR CARS IN 1989

'In 1989 in the United States we shifted from a producer-controlled automotive marketplace to a customer-driven marketplace, and we shall never return to the former. This is why customer satisfaction has become so important.' So spoke David Power of opinion researchers J.D. Power & Associates at a seminar in Germany. Power explained [1]:

> Near the end of the 1980s, we saw a fundamental structural change take place in the U.S. automotive market that has shocked and shaken our industry to its very bones. Customers took control for the first time. They began to exercise their freedom of choice. This was a difficult situation for management to understand, for they were production-focused men with successful backgrounds in engineering, production and finance.

Power believed that the phasing out of the Voluntary Restraint Agreement (VRA) restricting imports of Japanese cars was a significant event in this transition to a buyers' market. This action in America foreshadows future developments in Europe, where similar restraints are gradually being phased out during the 1990s and will end on 31 December 1999.

Most tragically, in Power's view, as late as 1991 the US car companies still thought that the American marketplace was producer-driven.

They were reluctant to give up the 'pile 'em high, sell 'em cheap' volume selling that had served them for decades. A prime example was GM's near-fatal reluctance to cut its capacity to suit its new lower market share. Here lies a clear warning to auto makers on other continents.

EUROPEAN SELLERS' MARKET ENDED IN 1990

The sellers' market for cars in Europe lasted for many decades. After World War II the demand for cars in Europe grew so quickly and steadily that life was easy for the auto producers. It was a sellers' market in which they could call the shots.

European car makers were living in a lavishly-furnished dream world. Europeans love cars and have been eager to buy them as their incomes have improved – indeed even in advance of their rising incomes. Since 1960 car ownership grew faster than the rate of increase of a key market-forming parameter, per-capita income. In the 30 years to 1990, GDP per capita grew by more than 138% in Europe while car ownership soared more than three times as fast by a spectacular 423%.

It was great while it lasted. But several exceptional years at the end of the 1980s only served to confirm the established views of many European industry leaders that they were sublime masters of their craft who were able to meet easily and profitably the transportation needs of European motorists. With rare exceptions, they could sell whatever they could build. Those who could not do so were in fact performing well below any reasonable industry standard.

An illusion of the continuation of the sellers' market in 1991 was created. The end of the boom was masked by record demand in Germany in 1991 fuelled by 12.7% growth in the former western Federal *Länder* and their reunification with Eastern Germany. The Eastern states absorbed a staggering 730 000 registrations or four times the volume of their new-car purchases in the last full year under Communist rule. But . . . this was only an illusion. The underlying trend was negative.

DIFFERING PERFORMANCES OF NATIONAL MARKETS

The braking of Europe's car-market growth has had a severe impact. In the British, Spanish and French economies, recession dragged 1991 auto demand down to the levels of 1987 and earlier. In other countries the sellers' market ended somewhat sooner. In the mid-1980s the Netherlands had already reached a cyclical stability around the half-million-car sales level. Other markets will follow the Dutch pattern as they approach quasi-saturation.

Mature in many characteristics, the Belgian, Irish, Luxembourg and Swiss markets are not expected to offer dynamic growth prospects.

Demand in four other markets – Finland, Sweden, Denmark and Norway – has so seriously deteriorated in the last few years that their car sales and distribution structures have come under severe stress. All suffer with sales at only half their recent peaks.

EUROPEAN WITHDRAWAL FROM EXPORT MARKETS

Adding to the problems of the European car makers in the 1990s was their gradual abandonment of export markets during the 1980s. Exports were a traditional buffer for excess production when home and European markets took breathers. With exports reduced, European production suffered disproportionately.

Accustomed to an easy life at home, the European producers became disillusioned with the wild fluctuations of the mature North American car market. Instead of persevering there they withdrew from the fickle and troublesome American continent. This reduced their ability to compensate abroad for slack sales periods at home. It also denied them the incentive and the means to learn how to cope with the challenge of a cyclical market – such as Europe is now becoming.

KEY FACTORS RESPONSIBLE FOR CHANGE

What put the buyer in the driver's seat? The following factors are chiefly responsible:

- **Overcapacity.** For at least a decade European car plants will have more production capacity than the market can absorb.
- **Wider Choice.** Thanks in part to the Japanese and other newcomers to Europe, a much wider selection of cars will be offered at attractive prices in all segments.
- **More Discerning Customers.** A more knowledgeable, better-informed and more-determined customer body is being created.
- **Dealer Freedom.** A progressive transition to a more liberalized system of distribution will give dealers more freedom of action and independence from their car suppliers.
- **Better-Quality Products.** The durability and reliability of all cars will improve further, so the quality of cars will be taken for granted. This will make their other attributes, such as design and performance, more important to buyers.

We discuss these and other contributing factors in this chapter and later in the book.

THE MENACE OF EXCESS CAPACITY

Looming on the horizon for the European manufacturers are the worrying consequences of the increasing Japanese industrial and market presence in Europe. The ambitions of the Korean producers must also be considered. The European marques sold 85% of their available production capacity in 1989. In 1990 this deteriorated to 83% when stocks built up and demand in the North American market declined. Worse followed and will continue to follow.

This is not to say that the European producers have been generous with capacity. Traditionally Europe's managers have preferred large order banks to large banks of cars in storage seeking buyers. Social rigidities have blocked the layoffs that the American producers employed to adjust output to demand in their cyclical markets. Now these rigidities have come to America as well in the form of the newest UAW contracts.

Thus in their golden high-growth years the European makers gained little experience of the profitable operation of plant facilities at less than capacity. In fact, they equipped their plants to suit their traditional production systems in ways that contributed little to manufacturing flexibility. The same rigidities also developed upstream in the suppliers to the industry, who became accustomed to long-running contracts for steady production volumes – conditions they may never see again.

TIME FOR DIFFICULT CAPACITY DECISIONS

Much of the improvement in GM's fortunes in Europe can be traced to its early action in closing plants and rationalizing (e.g. mothballing one of its Antwerp plants). This raised its effective use of capacity to levels approaching 100%. By introducing a virtual three-shift system in selected plants, GM achieved even higher utilization of its facilities.

But no one in Europe wants to be the first to flinch and cap or cut capacity permanently. Instead of the 'Big Six' car producers in Europe the 'Little Seven' were created by BMW's purchase of Rover. Each of these seven (not to mention Volvo and Mercedes-Benz) harbours dreams of seizing more market share at the expense of the others. To do this each needs capacity.

If all the plans to expand European capacity come to fruition and capacity withdrawals occur as expected, European manufacturers will increase their assembly capacity by 15.5% by 2000. This would be well ahead of a demand projection for their products which would expand by only 8% from 1989 levels.

This trend will profoundly affect the car manufacturers, their products and their profits. Someone, obviously, will suffer.

THE JAPANESE ARE INCREASING
EUROPE'S EFFICIENT CAPACITY

The complete picture for the European manufacturers requires consideration of the Japanese plans for extra capacity in Europe. Plants are

Fig. 1.1 The presence in Europe of Japanese production plants, such as this one of Honda's at Swindon, intensifies car industry competitiveness and contributes to the buyers' market.

already operated by Nissan in the United Kingdom and Spain, by Toyota and Honda in the UK, by Mitsubishi (with Volvo) in the Netherlands and by Suzuki in Spain and Hungary. Honda has had access to Rover facilities for its production and Mazdas are being produced by Ford in Britain.

Overall, we project an increase in Japanese transplant capacity from 1992 to 2000 of 1.4 million units, contributing nearly 40% of the total capacity increase planned in Europe [2]. These plants will dispense with old-style working practices, established trade-union structures and antiquated career expectations. The Japanese have already shown that they can improve upon the European system.

The indigenous Europeans also have expansion plans. Adding their new factories, but excluding Eastern European plants, Europe will gain a total additional assembly capacity for 3.7 million more cars by 2000. An estimate by the European Commission foresees capacity in excess of demand of at least 2 million units in the late 1990s and possibly as high as four and a half million units.

SLUGGISH EUROPEAN MARKET GROWTH FORECAST

Where will all these cars be sold? In the decade to 2000 the European manufacturers will experience no growth, and in some cases a significant reduction, in domestic demand for their products. This will result from reduced overall car demand and the annexation of a higher share of the market by Japanese and Korean brands.

In the 1990s, Euromotor Reports expects Europe's overall market growth to moderate from the 3.4% annual rate of the 1980s to a steadier pace of 2.4%, closer to the 2.6% annual rate achieved from 1970 to 1990 [2].

Through the 1990s, the proportion of the annual increase in registrations that will be captured by the Japanese will soar from under 20% to over 50%. The average for the period will find the Japanese annexing 45% of all additional sales from the base year of 1990.

What can be said of the market remaining for the European manufacturers? It will expand at the much lower average rate of 1.3–1.4% per annum over the decade. Even worse, this annual rate of market expansion for their sales will decrease through the period as Japanese transplant production accelerates.

EUROPE APPROACHING LIMITS OF MOTORIZATION DENSITY

The end of the sellers' market may also be related to trends in car-park sizes. The basic measure of car ownership, new or used, is the number of cars in service per 1000 population. On this ratio the USA is clearly the most motorized. In comparison to the USA, Europe operates some 20% fewer cars per head of population.

The highest European values are to be found in the four largest EU markets and in EFTA generally. The least-motorized markets, in order, are Greece, Portugal and Ireland. Japan, which has traditionally restricted car ownership and use at home, has a relatively low car density.

From 1981 to 1989 Europe's car density per 1000 population soared from 324 to 387, an increase of 19.4% [3]. Particularly striking was the accelerating car density in the Iberian peninsula, Finland and the United Kingdom. All these markets added cars at more than double the average rate for Europe.

More growth will come in Europe. The growth potential remains especially strong in Iberia and the new Central and Eastern Europe markets. But the overall trend of growth is shallow. More companies and cars are competing for Europe's growth. They are going all out to appeal to consumers to induce them to buy and remain faithful to their brand. They are acknowledging and acting on the change in Europe from a sellers' to a buyers' market.

EUROPE WILL COME TO RESEMBLE DUTCH AUTO MARKET

The reduced volume potential will give the entire European market the profile of a near-saturated marketplace for most of its participants.

Car marketing in the Netherlands, which we saw earlier was one of the first to achieve quasi-saturation, will suddenly resemble all too closely the general experience.

What are the Netherland's characteristics? Its relative sales stability, its reputation for orderly selling without some of the excesses of neighbouring Belgium and the UK, and its openness to all comers may mark this country as the future model for the marketer. In short, it was one of the first to become a buyers' market.

Risks to the future profitability of all participants in the supply channels are high. European manufacturers will be fighting to maintain sales in a less dynamic marketplace. They will also be confronted by more aggressive marketing by the formerly conservative Japanese marques. In combination, this shapes up as a classic buyers' market.

PULLING CARS THROUGH
INSTEAD OF PUSHING THEM THROUGH

Participants in the motor industry who are most aware of these changes realize that an historic transformation needs to take place in Europe. 'The industry is in the middle of a 180-degree change in the direction of its operations from "push" to "pull",' said consultant John Wormald [4]. 'This affects both its innovation and its delivery chains.' Wormald commented further:

> In the old dispensation, vehicle manufacturers structured their product lines around the scale-driven economics of lengthy design and development processes and of massive investments in hard automation. Production was to forecast and vehicle stocks were forced down through the distribution and dealership channel.

Now the industry needs to become responsive to customer demands and desires – an historic transition for Europe. 'The whole machine is increasingly now being made to run in reverse,' said Wormald, 'with operations responding as near as possible to real – as opposed to forecast – demand.' Many in the industry who have six speeds forward have only one speed in reverse. They're urgently trying to re-gear to meet the new conditions.

THE JAPANESE WILL COMPETE
MORE DIRECTLY WITH EUROPEANS

How will the Japanese respond to the change to a buyers' market? Restrictions on their imports to Europe will gradually be loosened. Now, the restrictions encourage a richer mix of products so more per-car revenue can be earned. With reduced restrictions, the Japanese will import cars that match the European range offerings more closely.

They are rightly renowned for their ability to understand and react to customer desires.

Additionally damaging to the Europeans will be the opportunity for the smaller Japanese marques, such as Honda, Mazda and Mitsubishi, to broaden their product ranges when volume levels permit. Being later arrivals in Europe, their allocations were restricted. Imported models were chosen to reflect the abilities of the available dealer network. During the 1990s these restraints will be relaxed.

These trends will offer customers a far greater selection of cars and car-like vehicles from which to choose. The European market already offers bewildering marque and product variety. This will only increase in the years ahead – to the benefit of the consumer and the frustration of the car marketer.

'PROFESSIONAL CUSTOMER'
A NEW MARKETPLACE FACTOR

Virtual saturation of the market in the USA contributed to its shift towards the buyers' market. At the same time, a more demanding consumer generation was created. Both in America and in Europe, the recession combined with increased leisure time and more intelligent shoppers to create a new breed of consumer, known as 'professional customers'. During the 1980s these professional customers were in the vanguard of the demand for better-quality goods. This is beginning to have a particularly strong impact in the automotive field.

MORE POWERFUL ROLES FOR WOMEN

Historically, women have been the pioneers in seeking out shopping bargains. Usually in control of the household budget, they have been leaders in demanding the best value for money spent.

Men, on the other hand, have been inclined to pay full list prices without bickering. They like to flaunt their spending as a sign of pride in their earning power. But now with many men finding it difficult to make ends meet in the recession, even they are beginning to be more cost-conscious.

Observers of the American scene have confirmed that more and more women are making car-buying decisions. They find women to be more rational and less emotional than men about the purchase of a car. Less motivated by ego-gratifying power and appearance factors, women respond more to rational ownership arguments. In particular they are concerned about car safety.

Similar trends are evident in Europe. In the western German states, for example, 21% of women drivers make the sole decision about the car they drive and an additional 33% participate in the buying decision [5]. Thus they influence more than half of new-car purchases.

OPTIMUM QUALITY ESSENTIAL
FOR CAR-MARKET ENTRY

In a poll conducted periodically in America by Roper, people select the most important reasons for buying a particular product brand. In 1985 quality led price as a motivation by 2 percentage points. In September 1992 price was more important than quality by 17 percentage points. However, this does not mean that quality has become less important; rather it means that the 'professional customers' are looking for top quality at the lowest price possible.

These intelligent, selective customers are less eager to pay the premium price that is charged by a major advertised brand. They know full well that if they pay that price they are paying quite a lot for the manufacturer's promotional efforts. As the quality of goods becomes more alike, these customers look sharply at price when making their buying decisions.

Independent surveys and those of governments show consistently that car quality is improving in all world markets, spurred by the high standard set by the Japanese producers since the 1970s. The Japanese took the view that 'business as usual' has to be a constant striving for perfection in the reliability and durability of their products. So strong is this trend that it is already threatening dealer and car-maker revenue from after-sales parts and service.

Thus simple functional quality is no longer an important differentiator between one brand and another. Quality simply must be good; it is the price of admission to the auto markets of today and tomorrow.

UNFINISHED SINGLE-MARKET
BUSINESS: CAR DISTRIBUTION

How the automotive industry sells its products to its customers and how these products are delivered and serviced will be profoundly affected by the progress made – or not made – in completing the European Single Market in the 1990s.

The car producers are granted the privileged status of selling and delivering their products through highly controlled distribution organizations. This right has been enshrined in the Motor Industry Selective Distribution Block Exemption, granted by the European Commission in mid-1985 for a 10-year life span and renewed, in amended form, in 1995.

Under the Regulation the franchised-dealer distribution system is exempted from the terms of the Treaty of Rome, which tolerates no discrimination in the distribution of any products in the EU. Without the exemption, car makers would be unable to oblige their dealers to sell their brands exclusively or to restrict their sales of cars to certain regions or categories of retailers.

SELECTIVE DISTRIBUTION SYSTEM UNDER FIRE

This car distribution system has been under fire from consumer groups and from some political entities as working against the best interests of the consumer. It is seen by them as being contrary to both the spirit and the letter of the rules of open competition within the Single Market.

The European Commission has evaluated the way the auto companies have been supplying the market under the Block Exemption and have adopted a new Regulation for the period after July 1995. It is concerned with such matters as:

- real and effective competition between marques in a national and international sense;
- pricing and commercial terms across national boundaries;
- product availability within the Single Market.

So far the car industry has argued successfully and, in our view, soundly and justifiably, that the sale and service of a complex product like a car, with obvious safety implications, demands a franchised network that is able to support trained service requirements with the profits made from sales. The European Commission has closely observed the industry to see whether this linkage continues to be both needed and implemented by the car makers and their dealers.

CUSTOMER SATISFACTION IS KEY FUTURE ISSUE

The EU's Competition Directorate has shifted the balance of power somewhat more towards dealers in its new Regulation. It has granted to dealers more freedom to take on another car maker's franchise within their contract territory. Dealers now will participate in mutually setting sales targets and establishing quotas for vehicle stocks and demonstrators. Arbitration procedures could be used to resolve differences between car makers and their dealers.

To the extent that they are embodied in a new Regulation such provisions will increase the ability of dealers to represent better their end customers to the factory. Dealers will be less obliged to follow every dictate of their suppliers. This will give car buyers an opportunity to benefit from these changes in the retail structure.

Accentuated competition inter- and intra-brand will result, bringing keener prices and enhanced value for money. Thus customer satisfaction is at the heart of one of the most critical issues facing Europe's car industry.

EVIDENCE THAT
CUSTOMER SATISFACTION SUPPORTS SALES

The core issue for car marketers must be whether or not the achievement of high customer satisfaction will help them compete more effectively in a buyers' market. Some anecdotal evidence suggests that it will. The evidence is especially strong in America, where the customer has been king since 1989.

Close correlation between high customer satisfaction and competitiveness in the marketplace is suggested by the performance of the Japanese upscale brand names in the USA. The sales achievements of the Lexus, Infiniti and Acura franchises indicate that high customer satisfaction indices (CSI) and strong sales growth are positively associated. All three marques regularly achieve Top-10 listings in the CSI surveys carried out by the J.D. Power organization and, at the same time, have been successful in penetrating the US luxury-car market.

Car manufacturers in North America have carried out wide-ranging surveys to determine the impact of improved CSI ratings on business success. They have concluded that for auto dealers and their salesforce a high CSI is one of the keys to sales success. As a result they are beginning to recommend bonus allocations on the basis of CSI ratings as well as sales. Whether or not this is a good idea we will discuss later.

Fig. 1.2 With its Lexus range Toyota set new standards for customer satisfaction, according to American CSI surveys, that have contributed to their sales successes.

QUANTIFYING THE LINK
BETWEEN SATISFACTION AND SALES

'Customer satisfaction is at its highest level when the guy gets his new car,' Bob Marshall, Ford's Executive Director of Corporate Quality, told Lindsay Brooke [6]. 'After that, it deteriorates.' What counts most comes later: how satisfied are owners with their choice of brand when the time comes to choose a new car?

As an example, Bob Marshall said that if Ford's initial 90% satisfaction levels were to plunge to 50% after four years, only half Ford's owners would give any priority to Ford as their next supplier. 'If you could somehow keep that up to 80% after four years,' added Marshall, 'you're going to conquest your competition. If people are happy with their car over an extended period, they form an affection for the car and an affection for the company. And that gives you a hell of an edge on their loyalty.'

KEY TO SUCCESS IN A BUYERS' MARKET:
CUSTOMER SATISFACTION

Is the concept of 'brand loyalty' still valid in the increasingly fickle marketplace of the 1990s? If so, who is responsible for building brand loyalty? Is it the car maker or is it the dealer?

Brand identities and reputations are chiefly made or broken by the manufacturers. The power to establish the credibility behind any brand or product statement must lie with the car makers. But are the auto makers doing the best they can in this context while still depending on their dealers to make major efforts to comply with customer-satisfaction guidelines?

Customer satisfaction is the vital link with continued success in a competitive marketplace. This was emphasized by a study for the British Department of Trade and Industry on manufacturing in the 1990s. As one of its four main themes it identified higher consumer expectations [7]: 'Customer power continues to grow and to compete effectively you must satisfy existing and new customers profitably.' True for all industries, this is especially important to auto makers.

Customerization is capable of guiding all the actions of a company and its dealers, as the following chapters will show. But the auto industry is still learning how to apply this concept most effectively, especially in Europe. Those who use it first and best will gain an important one-time advantage over their present and future rivals.

RECAPTURING 'CUSTOMERS'
FROM THE MASS OF 'CONSUMERS'

The word 'customer' is used advisedly in this book instead of another that might have been used: 'consumer'. Stephen Bayley comments on the difference [8]:

> The term 'consumer' had come into use as a description of bourgeois economic activity in the eighteenth century. In the new markets of the rapidly industrialising nations, making and using became known as producing and consuming. It is interesting to chart the relative decline of the old-fashioned, more genteel word 'customer' against the rise of the more abstract, aggressive 'consumer'.
>
> The history of the word 'consumer' reveals the development of the Western economy. Mass production and all that it entails – investment, long lead times, low unit costs and ready availability – replaced a system where simple makers could articulate and satisfy needs; the new distant customers alienated from the production process became consumers.

No clearer explanation of the need to rehabilitate and enshrine the word 'customer' could be written. Bayley emphasizes the point by saying, 'Semantically, "customer" suggests familiarity and regularity and a one-to-one relationship with a retailer or a manufacturer, while the remote "consumer" is a more relevant, impersonal tag in global markets giddy with excess.' We are aiming to put aside the 'mass' view of the marketplace and focus instead on the desires of the individual customer.

THE CUSTOMER AS THE MEASURE
OF ALL CAR-INDUSTRY ACTIVITY

We hold the view that consideration of the customer's needs and desires can and should pervade every aspect of conceiving, creating, making, selling and servicing cars. Our aim will be to use the advice and guidance of the customer in making every decision and taking every action.

If we are successful, we will please and keep our customers for our products and services. Broadly, this book will discuss this in terms of customer 'satisfaction'. Some will stress the need to go beyond mere satisfaction in order to 'delight' or 'excite' the customer. These too are worthy goals; we will discuss how they are being achieved. They make clear that there is no limit to the effort we can make to improve the relationship between company and customer – any more than there are limits to the quality of the relationship between two people.

In some areas this may seem difficult. How, for example, in car manufacturing can we be in contact with the end customer? How can advertising speak to the individual rather than the mass? Dealers seems to have the heaviest customer-facing burden; how are they to cope with it? We demonstrate the validity of customerizing – and its profitable application – in the following chapters.

POINTS FOR DISCUSSION AND REVIEW

- When did Europe become a buyers' market for cars and why?
- Name three factors contributing to excess capacity in the car industry.
- Why does the Dutch auto market forecast the future for Europe?
- What characteristics do women display as purchasers of cars?
- Does functional quality still provide important differentiation between car brands?
- What is the difference between 'consumers' and 'customers'?

Reason for urgency: car business transformation 2

Customerization needs to be implemented urgently throughout the car business. It is not a 'management tool' that you have the option of adopting, it is an imperative for future success: how you implement it in your work and organization is up to you. We hope to provide some ideas in this book. But customerization brooks no delay.

Urgent action is needed because the buyers' market is upon us all with a vengeance and will be with us, in greater or lesser degrees, indefinitely. This fact alone has produced pockets of crisis-level problems in our industry. In this chapter we discuss the nature and the seriousness of these crises to emphasize that immediate action is needed to speed the customerization of all car businesses.

First we raise and answer the question: why does it matter? Of what importance is this industry anyway?

THE HUGE IMPORTANCE OF THE CAR BUSINESS

Considering Europe alone, the production, distribution and sales of cars generate the second most important economic activity after the food and drink industry. They create more than 10% of Europe's gross national product and employ directly or indirectly more than 11% of its workforce.

We assess the total European new-car-sales turnover at the end of the 1980s at Ecu 161 billion, of which the company-fleet share was some Ecu 29 billion. Private consumers would therefore have been spending 40–42% of their total consumption of transportation needs on new cars [3].

New-car retailing is thus a vast economic activity by any standard. New-car sales in Europe in 1989, including taxes, exceeded the value of the individual Gross Domestic Product (GDP) of 11 nations in Europe. The entire Dutch national economy was only 3% larger than the new-car sales value of the car industry in the 17 markets of the European Economic Area (EEA).

These figures only hint at the total economic value of the car sector.

End-1980s used-car sales throughout Europe were estimated to be worth more than Ecu 86 billion and parts and service combined amounted to some Ecu 57 billion. Therefore in final-customer terms the passenger-car sector was worth more than Ecu 305 billion, rising to Ecu 324 billion in 1991.

TRANSPORTATION AND CAR SHARES OF INCOMES

We can also look at the sector from a broader perspective. After food and housing costs, Europeans spend more on transportation than on any other budget item. The average European dedicates 15% of their total spending to personal transportation.

What share of this spending goes to cars? From average car prices and car operating expenditures, Euromotor Reports Ltd calculate that cars absorb between 77% and 84% of the total transportation bill. Thus car ownership takes some 11–12% of all household expenditure in Europe.

This indicates an outlay of Ecu 320–50 billion in 1989 and an estimated Ecu 337–70 billion in 1991 [3]. Included are all the heavy taxes and duties that are levied on this fiscally productive (and fiscally burdened) economic sector.

DECLINING IMPORTANCE OF PARTS AND SERVICE

What trends can we identify in the ways this money is spent? One trend is important: car maintenance requirements are falling. Service intervals are now often set at 12 000 miles, rather than the 3000 and 5000 miles that were typical in 1980. The workshop time for each service has also been reduced. A major service would often exceed 4.5 hours early in the decade but by 1990 this had typically been reduced to 3.0 hours or less.

Improved car reliability and these extended service intervals are reducing parts and service revenue. Launching its new 800 in late 1991, Rover highlighted servicing cost savings as a major selling point for the car: service would cost 20% less for the first 60 000 miles than for the previous model.

If consumers keep their service savings in their auto budgets, their new-car purchases could increase. On the other hand the car makers, knowing full well what these trends mean for dealer gross revenues and their own income, could be tempted to push car prices upward ahead of general retail prices to recoup net income when their other revenues decline.

REDUCING ENERGY CONSUMPTION
IN MAKING AND SCRAPPING CARS

Another area of concern is the total energy consumption of the car, through manufacturing as well as use. Car production and eventual scrappage account for no more than 10–15% of the total energy consumed during the life of the car. Operation and servicing consume 85–90% of the total energy used.

In practical terms this means that any design effort put into ensuring easy recoverability of materials must have the criterion of weight saving as a first priority, to improve fuel economy. Putting it differently, the use of plastics in cars to reduce weight must not be curtailed just because plastics account for a major part of the growing scrappage problem created by cars at the ends of their lifetimes.

Thus concerns about car scrappage and recycling must still be secondary to the main issue of growing car use and ever-higher fuel consumption. Programmes to build and then dismantle more-recyclable cars will take 15–20 years to implement fully, which postpones their benefits for a generation. In contrast, a further reduction of 10% in the already-good European average fleet fuel consumption, if implemented by January 1997, would have more energy benefit by 2000 than any recycling successes.

STRONG SINGLE-MARKET IMPACT ON AUTO BUSINESSES

As the largest single manufacturing industry in the EU, motor-vehicle production and distribution will be significantly affected by changes in the Union's structure. That is an opinion shared by those who do business in the EU. In an EU-wide survey, 11 000 EU businesspeople ranked the motor-vehicle industry highest in terms of the importance to it of the removal of technical barriers to trade.

The Single Market is bound to encourage growth, although its success depends on factors other than economic growth. For example it will depend on attitudes to cars generally and on conservation considerations. The large and growing EU market will still offer major opportunities to European car and component manufacturers.

The EU has also attracted considerable Japanese interest and investment. Having a significant impact in the 1990s, this will influence even more the post-2000 motor market in Europe. The genie, once released from the bottle, is not easily persuaded to return.

SALES AND REGISTRATIONS BECOMING CYCLICAL

Europe's new-car registrations have been in a slump from 1989's high of just under 13.5 million vehicles. The 1990 total dropped to 13.3 million cars. On a comparable basis 1991 fell further to 12.8 million cars. The one-time boost of some 0.8 million registrations in the former East Germany meant that 1991 produced an artificial sales 'record' slightly over 13.5 million cars.

The downward trend resumed in 1992 with the total registration of 13.4 million cars in the new Western Europe. It continued in 1993 when registrations slumped to less than 11.4 million units, followed by a small rise to 11.9 million cars registered in 1994.

Assisted by a gradual upturn in economic trends, the world automotive industry is now entering a period of sales recovery. Global volumes were higher in 1994 than in 1993 and 1995 figures are higher still in the nine major manufacturing nations. But our key conclusion must be that Europe is entering, for the first time, a period of cyclical sales fluctuations that render near-term forecasting virtually impossible.

PRODUCTION AND PROFITABILITY BOTH DOWN

After years of steady rises that seemed God-ordained, production of cars in Western Europe fell for the second year in succession in 1991. The total of 13.1 million cars produced was 3.5% down on 1990, which itself saw a 0.9% decline from 1989. Production fell further to 12.9 million in 1992 and to 11.0 million in 1993. Only a slight rise was recorded in 1994.

Figures for production in the EU show a parallel picture. From a high of 13.3 million units in 1989 output plummeted to only 11.0 million in 1993. By 1996 output is forecast to recover in the EU to the 1989 level. By 1999 it is expected to rise further to a new record of 16.0 million units, helped by strong growth in the UK, aided by the Japanese producers, and in Italy.

The early-1990s declines in car sales and production dramatically reversed the steady rises of the late 1980s. Although decision makers in Europe's car industry knew the boom years would end, they were poorly prepared for the downturn when it came. As a result, the overall profit margins of the industry suffered badly.

The deterioration of European vehicle manufacturers' financial performance during the recession of the past few years has been serious. Of the 'Big Six' automotive manufacturers in Europe, PSA – Volkswagen, Renault, Fiat, Ford and GM – only Renault and GM made a profit in 1993.

Although 1994 was better, the severe losses experienced in the industry in Europe have encouraged its effort to restructure businesses in an effort to return to profitability. For that restructuring, customerization is an important criterion.

HARSH AND CONTINUING IMPACTS ON JOBS

Job cuts have followed the industry's decline. From the German car industry's all-time-high employment of 788 000 in July 1991, more than 50 000 were lost in 1992. The year 1993 saw a cut of a further 60 000 jobs. Cutbacks in the German workforce were suspended during 1994. As of December 1994 the German auto industry employed 655 000 people, 20 000 less than in December 1993, a fall of 17% from the peak.

This may only be the beginning. Some analysts hold that by the end of the century Germany should be employing no more than 350 000 auto workers – almost half the current level. Dr Erika Emmerich, President of the VDA, is on record as saying [9] 'the German automobile industry must urgently improve its competitiveness, if it intends to keep and confirm its position on the world market.'

GERMANY'S LEADING FIRMS ARE RESTRUCTURING

Even Germany's best performer, BMW, has not escaped the impact of the crisis. Deliveries to its distributors fell in 1993 for the first time since 1974 before recovering in 1994. In addition, BMW's turnover has been hurt by currency devaluations in some export markets and by the increased share of sales accounted for by the 3-Series models which sell at lower prices.

The car operations of Daimler-Benz are feeling the pressure too. Said the company's Chairman through mid-1995, Edzard Reuter, 'the German economy burst like a soap bubble'. Mercedes-Benz cut its workforce by 14 700 in Germany in 1992, by another 11 000 in 1993 and shed nearly 10 000 more workers by the end of 1994. Across its car and commercial-vehicle divisions Mercedes-Benz reduced its workforce by over 18% by the end of 1994.

Severe restructuring is also on the cards at Volkswagen. Volkswagen AG has shed 27 000, a quarter of its employees, over the last five years. Yet increased productivity has left the VW Group with an excess of 30 000 employees in Germany in 1994. In order to preserve employment levels VW has agreed a package with the unions to cut both wages and working hours substantially.

It is clear that the company still has more work to do. Indeed its Chairman, Mr Ferdinand Piëch, said in June 1995: 'The short-lived bush fire has been put out and all that is left is a battle for prices and market share of the sort that we have never seen before in Germany.'

JOB CUTS IN OTHER EUROPEAN NATIONS

The VDA's Dr Emmerich referred to [9] 'the profound structural change which is gripping the automobile industry not only in Germany but also worldwide.' Battening down its hatches over the last three years in France, Citroën has cut its workforce by more than 10% to 29 000 while Peugeot has made similar cuts in its domestic workforce, which now totals 52 000.

Over 15 000 Ford of Europe employees have left that company since 1992. In the Netherlands NedCar has slashed its workforce by 20%, eliminating 1200 of its 5400 jobs. This was in addition to cuts of almost 4000 jobs since 1990 to prepare the company for fresh investment from its two owners, Volvo and Mitsubishi. Volvo Car's own workforce fell by one fifth between 1990 and 1993 but has risen by 8% in 1994 over 1993 to reach 29 000.

PERMANENT CHANGE TO NEW BUSINESS CONDITIONS

Our aim in recounting these problems of the European car industry is not to suggest that it will never see good times again. We intend rather to point out that the industry is entering a new and less settled era in which completely different conditions apply and will continue to apply. These conditions require early and sharp adaptations to greater responsiveness and flexibility by all participants in the industry.

A senior executive at PSA highlighted one of these problems when he told us that he was worried about the ultimate impact of the Single Market because it could cause the entire European market to cycle up and down in volume in unison – like the American market – instead of helping car makers maintain their volumes by balancing falls in some countries with rises in others. For this and the other reasons explained earlier, Europe is heading for more cyclicality. Booms we will have, and busts as well.

Other changes as mentioned in Chapter 1 are also permanent: increased competition from more brands and models, a need for increased cost efficiency to compete with imports and rebuild exports, heavy pressure on car and component development costs, increased retail dealer independence and authority and the creation of a more demanding customer body. None of these will reverse or is reversible. These new conditions will prevail indefinitely.

THE CUSTOMER WILL BE THE RESCUER

GM's Louis Hughes said about the problems of the car business, 'News from the executioner concentrates the mind.' We have all heard the news from the executioner. Europe's industry is at a critical juncture, and in this it is not alone in the world. The problems are well illustrated by this brief review of facts that are becoming all too evident.

Our objective in this book is to introduce the person who will be what the Germans call *der Retter in der Not*, the rescuer in the hour of need. In fact, the rescuer will not be one single person. Rather, it will be the most important person in your organizations: your customer.

Customers will rescue us. They will lead auto businesses out of the crisis and towards great future success. That is, they will if we let them! For some companies, and particularly for some people in them, handing over the controls of their business to the customer will represent one of the most difficult challenges that they have ever faced.

POINTS FOR DISCUSSION AND REVIEW

- What should have priority in car materials selection and why: fuel economy or recycling?
- Discuss the characteristics of Germany's car industry and its importance to the German economy.
- Do improving sales volumes mean that the auto industry has put its problems behind it?
- Name some of the effects of Europe's Single Market on its car industry.
- What factors are affecting the car industry's profits from parts and service sales?

3 Customer-driven car research and development

Research and development (R&D) begins at the very moment of conception of a new kind of car. Like human conception, this occurs under conditions of utmost secrecy. How, then, can the customer be considered? How can the customer be present when decisions are made about the types of vehicles offered and the features they will include?

The answer is that the car's creators must act on behalf of the customer. They must stand in as personal surrogates for him and her when and where the key decisions are made. Even more importantly, they must envision what customers would most like to have – even when the customers themselves don't know. Therein lies the essential art of motor industry success.

'There is no substitute for fabulous products,' said Keith Magee, the head of Ford's Lincoln-Mercury Division [10]. 'The Mercury Villager is a good example. We've brought a lot of people into L-M stores who had never been there before because of Villager. Sure, advertising was good, and we offered good value, but you can't ever underestimate the value of product. Customers want great products.'

INTENSIFIED COMPETITION IN GROWING HIGH-VALUE SEGMENTS

The broadest theme of the conception of great products concerns the ranges and types of vehicles a company will seek to offer. In the 1990s the Japanese producers have been making the running in expanding their ranges to compete by adding special-purpose products. Vehicles such as the minivan, the sports car and recreational vehicles in the 4×4 category make great contributions to their success.

By 1990 the Japanese had won over 50% of the market in each of these three specialist areas. And these segments are forecast to grow. We expect the market for two-seater sports cars to expand from 40 000 to 70 000 by 2000, a 75% increase. The 4×4 market will double

Fig. 3.1 The Chrysler T-115 (1995 Town & Country model here) exemplified the challenge of innovating R&D for a market that 'isn't there'. Chrysler built it and buyers came.

to 400 000 new units in 2000 and minivans will surge 220% from today's 250 000 to 800 000 units by 2000. This is growth no car maker can ignore.

IMPORT RESTRAINTS
INCREASE JAPANESE INTEREST IN NEW SEGMENTS

While they remain in effect through the 1990s, the terms of the agreed restraints on exports by the Japanese manufacturers will actually intensify their resolve to compete in the smaller, high-value segments that were previously 'reserved' for the luxury and specialist suppliers, especially those in Europe.

Toyota's Lexus and Honda's Acura were precursors of what is intended to be a major upmarket reorientation of imported Japanese ranges. Mazda's Eunos/Xedos and Nissan's Infiniti have been launched to follow as high-prestige product lines that complement their respective volume ranges. That some of these are less successful than others does not invalidate the soundness of their long-term plans.

At the same time the Japanese companies will seek to gain a competitive advantage by whole-product innovation that will create new niches that have the potential to grow into segments. New-segment creators have a massive advantage over their rivals in the amount of time they have for the exploitation of the advantages of their new concept.

It can take years for the opposition to put rival products into the marketplace; meanwhile the whole-product innovator is reaping the rewards. They are selling a vehicle that cannot be price-compared against its competition because it has no direct competition.

HOW DO YOU INNOVATE
FOR A MARKET THAT 'ISN'T THERE'?

The importance of generating new product ideas to gain business success was underlined by Austrian Michael Brandtner [11]:

> The real art of marketing is not to please the individual but to attract the mass. And there is only one way: new ideas, not new instruments. All big marketing successes were built first upon ideas, as was the case with Apple, Nike and Sega. Without ideas first, all marketing efforts, from mass advertising to database marketing, are not worth the paper they are written on.

The best example of a whole-product innovation, called a 'chartbuster' by GM because it creates a new island on the product chart, is not Japanese but American: the front-drive Chrysler T-115 minivan. It was based on a concept which product planner Hal Sperlich tried

Fig. 3.2 By creating its EV-50 concept car and displaying it at motor shows Toyota tested the water for a new kind of small sport-utility vehicle. It evolved into the RAV4.

to advance when he worked at Ford, without success. Chrysler, much in need of new product, adopted both Sperlich and the concept and profited hugely from that decision.

Said Sperlich about Ford [12]:

> They lacked confidence that a market existed, because the product didn't exist. The auto industry places great value on historical studies of market segments. Well, we couldn't prove that there was a market for the minivan because there was no historical segment to cite.
>
> Thus in Detroit most product-development dollars are spent on modest improvements to existing products and most market research money is spent studying what customers like among available products. In 10 years of developing the minivan we never once got a letter from a housewife asking us to invent one. To the sceptics, that proved there wasn't a market out there.

In 1994 another whole-product innovation was introduced to the market by Toyota: the RAV4. This is the company's first attempt at a chartbuster, the first time, as *Car Styling* said, that Toyota 'came to experience the excitement and "anxiety" of venturing onto the niche market'. Toyota hopes that the RAV4's combination of a passenger-car's structure and cost with a sport-utility's looks and drive train will create a niche which it can exploit.

Fig. 3.3 Toyota minimized the risk attendant upon the launch into a speculative niche of its RAV4 'new-concept' 4×4, based on the EV-50, by using many components already in production.

'IMAGINEERING' IS THE ANSWER

The RAV4 was the result of free thinking about a vehicle that would drive comfortably both on and off the road, refined in two successive Tokyo Show concept cars. Hal Sperlich conceived the Chrysler minivan by watching the way people used their cars and thinking about a product that could be helpful to them. A successful innovator, he answered the question that consumers would have asked – if they could have.

Sony Corporation has derived much of its success from a similar ability to 'imagineer' the unspoken desires of customers. 'Reengineering' advocates Michael Hammer and James Champy write [13], 'When Sony developers first envisioned the Walkman, management did not order up a market research survey to see if the product would be embraced by customers. Realizing that people are unable to conceptualize what they do not know, Sony gave the Walkman the green light based on developers' instincts into people's needs and the capabilities of technology.'

Getting and using ideas demands relentless forward movement. Richard Branson of Virgin Atlantic says that ideas and opportunities are like London buses. If you spend your time wondering why you missed the last one, you miss the next one. Says Branson, 'If you really want to motivate staff in any business you have to create the best product – a product they are proud to be part of. Then the number one skill is to praise, praise and praise your staff.'

CREATING CHANCES FOR CHARTBUSTERS

Although he is no enemy of conventional market research if it is correctly and thoroughly done, productivity guru W. Edwards Deming took the view that the customer will ultimately render judgement on a new idea but that idea will probably not originate with the customer [14]:

> Innovation to invent new product and new service has been accomplished in every case in my experience by application of innovation and knowledge. A consumer can seldom say today what new product or new service would be desirable and useful to him three years from now, or a decade from now.
>
> New product and new types of service are generated, not by asking the consumer, but by knowledge, imagination, innovation, risk, trial and error on the part of the producer, backed by enough capital to develop the product or service and to stay in business during the lean months of introduction.

The critical word here is 'risk'. Chrysler was willing to take the risk that the T-115 answered an unspoken need. Sony took the same risk with the Walkman. Any visitor to a Japanese superstore will see many other electronic products which represent an investment in risk – products looking for customers. Many will not succeed. But those that do succeed have a chance to win big and to have a true niche market to themselves for some time. They have a chance to be 'chartbusters'.

Not all ideas will make the grade. One of Britain's most prolific inventors, Sir Clive Sinclair, is known equally well for his successes and his failures. Asked about the failures, Sir Clive said, 'It was just one of those things. If you want to invent you have to take the failures with the successes.'

JAPANESE ARE ACCEPTING SOME LIMITS

The opportunities for new automotive products are not unlimited, however. Even the Japanese are concluding that they have overstepped the bounds of desirable product proliferation. They may have taken note of the fate of their motorcycle industry, which hurled new models at its customers so explosively that they collapsed from sheer exhaustion and bewilderment.

'Toyota has made an extensive effort to be number one in customer satisfaction,' the company's Ryuji Araki told *Automotive News* [15]. 'But maybe we overdid it. We have been obsessed with it. On leather seats, for example, we would eliminate parts of the skin that contained natural blemishes, such as marks from insect bites. That was too much.'

Automotive News reporters Maskery and Johnson see Toyota as looking even more closely at the parameters of customer satisfaction to be sure that it is not overdoing its R&D effort to the detriment of its profitability:

> Toyota's efforts to redefine customer satisfaction are part of an overall cost-cutting campaign that is the most massive the company has ever undertaken. As Toyota pulls back from the excesses of the 1980s, it also is attempting to reduce model variations – or trim levels – by 20% and cut the number of different parts the company uses by 30%. So is 'average' now good enough? Maybe. The focus at Toyota now, according to Araki, is 'value' and a 'proper and reasonable' level of quality.

'PRODUCT CHURNING' BY JAPANESE WILL CONTINUE

Japan's auto industry, reports Christopher Lorenz [16], may be 'about to drop one of its most vicious competitive weapons: "product churning"'.

> This is the practice of launching a bewildering flood of new and face-lifted products at ever-shorter intervals. Its advantages are

that distribution channels are kept full; consumers are constantly beguiled with novelties, and – most important – the churner's competitors barely get a look-in.

The most authoritative western source on product churning is the consultant credited with inventing the term, Kevin Jones of McKinsey & Company, who has lived in Japan for a decade. 'Product churning won't stop – it has become part of the corporate woodwork and is now a necessary competitive tool,' he says. 'On the other hand, it probably will not accelerate any further.'

Rather than dropping product churning, Jones forecasts that manufacturers will keep it at its current level and add three further weapons to it.

These weapons are, says Lorenz:

1. Even greater productivity in research, design and development.
2. The injection of more really new content and added value into their 'new' products.
3. A smattering of western project-evaluation techniques, at least at relatively elevated levels in the corporate hierarchy.

Except at a few companies the middle managers involved in regular product development and launch decisions tend not to possess the financial skills necessary to calculate returns on investment in individual new products, or even in entire product lines. Development and launch decisions are based on simpler principles, such as market leadership, beating the competition and supporting distribution channels.

FILLING CURRENT CUSTOMER NEEDS IS NOT ENOUGH

When he was Ford's Chairman of the Board, Donald E. Petersen used Edward Deming's principles to energize his company's product development in the 1980s. He also stressed the need to look beyond the limited horizon of the present customer [17]:

When you're developing a product or a service, you have to look beyond what the average customer says he wants to things he doesn't even know he can have. He doesn't know he can have them because he hasn't seen or heard of them. Coming up with features like this is quite a challenge, but it is absolutely essential if you hope to stay ahead of the competition. If you deliver only what the customer wants at the moment, somebody else is going to blow you away with something that goes beyond your product or service in quality or innovation.

An engineer at Ford's great rival, GM, also underlined the importance of reaching out beyond everyday expectations to deliver the exceptional: 'If we hope to recapture market share we can only do it by exciting our customer. One of the ways to do that is by giving him more than he expected. Value excites customers.'

CONCEPTS MUST SATISFY BY MEETING UNEXPRESSED DESIRES

Chrysler too is given credit for discovering and acting upon the principle that customers must be surprised and delighted by the product. 'Chrysler Corp.'s cab-forward design in its LH cars not only offers wider doors for easier entry and exit and better visibility in the front but it also gives passengers in the back enormous leg room,' reported Bruce Nussbaum [18]. 'Passengers have been known to tap the driver on the shoulder to express their surprise.

'Designing to surprise the customer is the least understood factor in designing for hit products,' Nussbaum added. 'But that extra delight may provide just what is needed to push a good-selling product into the stratosphere.' In other words, surprise and pleasure in unexpected added value makes the difference between ordinary and exceptional customer acceptance – and marketplace performance.

CAN DEALERS PLAY A CREATIVE ROLE?

In individual cases retail dealers have made important contributions to R&D in the car industry. For Ford in the USA, Bob Tasca in Rhode Island was an indefatigable enthusiast supporting the development of better products. So was Jim Wangers at Royal Pontiac for that GM division. Germany's Auto-Becker in Düsseldorf has been a strong promoter and encourager of new vehicle concepts.

These, however, are the exceptions. Auto companies are suspicious of dealers who take too much interest in the product. They view them as dilettantes and suggest that they are 'probably not spending enough time on the business'. This could change, of course. Enlightened car makers could stop discouraging and start encouraging dealers to participate more in the product process. But few dealers will be qualified to do so.

The situation is different in Japan, where substantial strata of dealerships are company-owned. Often central staff and R&D personnel work in such dealerships, either to accelerate sales in slow periods or to gather personal impressions of customer desires. In the Tokyo area the major Japanese producers have set up multi-storey entertainment-cum-sales centres to attract younger buyers and learn their preferences directly. Toyota has added such a centre in Osaka.

Generally, MIT researchers reported [19], in the American and European systems the independent retail dealers:

have almost no link with the sales and marketing divisions, which are responsible for moving the metal. The dealer's skills lie in persuasion and negotiation, not in feeding back information to the product planners.

Moreover, a dealer has little incentive to share any information on customers with the manufacturer. The dealer's attitude is, 'What happens in my showroom is my business.'

We consider that dealers are entirely justified in taking this view.

JAPANESE DESIGNERS CONDUCT RESEARCH PERSONALLY

The record shows that in the modern era the Japanese car makers have pioneered the direct, personal, market-sensitive approach to innovative R&D. Author Eric Taub relates how [20] 'the now-ubiquitous cupholder was introduced into Japanese cars after a research team travelled the California freeways and noticed that many drivers drank coffee while on the road. The idea didn't come from a driver's suggestion, but from an executive's observation.'

In a similar vein, Robert Shook reported on the practical way in which Honda's designers attacked a problem in North America [21]: 'A US Honda design team, stalemated on a trunk design project, spent an afternoon in a Disneyland parking lot observing what people put into and took out of their car trunks and what kind of motion was involved. It was a classic example of on-the-spot research. Honda didn't hire an outside market research firm to provide stacks of data about trunk usage. They took a more direct approach and ultimately came up with a new design.'

Honda's hands-on approach also contributed to the worldwide sales success of the Civic. Robert Shook again [21]:

> In the late 1960s, shortly after the company began manufacturing automobiles, Soichiro Honda announced that he wanted to make a 'world car'. To accomplish this, the company sent two teams of engineers to travel around the world to collect data about products and life-styles of people in other countries.
>
> In conjunction with this programme, Honda's R&D sent engineers to Europe with instructions to spend a full year there doing nothing but observing the relationship between the citizens of those countries and their automobiles. The engineers studied everything from road conditions to driving habits. Then they returned to Japan to report their findings. This information helped Honda to design the first Civic.

Fig. 3.4 The creation of the original Honda Civic was the result of the vision of Soichiro Honda that his company was capable of producing a new model that would enjoy world success.

GM ENGINEERS TAKING RESEARCH INTO THEIR OWN HANDS

In 1993 *Automotive Industries* asked GM engineers for their candid views on what the company could be doing better. It discovered that the engineers weren't waiting to be told to make their own studies of the marketplace; they were doing so on their own initiative because they no longer trusted the marketing guidance they were given [22]:

> If the marketing guy is big and fat and smokes cigars, you can bet the car will have a tilt wheel and a huge ashtray. It won't matter if the car is targeted at women who don't smoke; the marketing guy will only think of himself.
>
> The marketing guy knows one thing – how to market for mass production. That's important – I'm not saying it isn't, but today it's only half the picture. In today's market you have to learn to adapt your thinking for smaller and niche markets.
>
> If we as engineers really want to know what's going on, we don't listen to the marketing guy, we look at the real world. We go to competitive dealerships to see what our target customer is buying and why. We shouldn't have to do that but we can't trust our internal information.

In fact, they *should* have to do that. Data is good but hands-on contact with the product, the dealer, the showroom and the customer is better. Frustrated, GM's engineers are finding this out for themselves. Doing so will help them reach into the mind and heart of the customer.

CURRENT OWNERS
CAN MAKE IMPORTANT CONTRIBUTIONS

Where customers are personally involved in the earliest stages of the research to define a new product, the approaches taken by various companies can differ sharply. Opinion research surveys and product clinics are often spread broadly over a sampling of the entire spectrum of car owners to sweep up as large a body of potential buyers as possible.

In contrast, said the authors of the report on MIT's International Motor Vehicle Program [19]: 'Toyota went directly to its existing customers in planning new products. Established customers were treated as members of the "Toyota Family" and brand loyalty became a salient feature of Toyota's lean production system.'

Chrysler listened successfully to members of its owner family when it planned the second-generation major facelift of the T-115 minivan. Owners enjoyed using this unique vehicle – so much so that they took the time to write to Chrysler to make suggestions on the way it could be improved. Chrysler read their letters and followed their suggestions. The result: continuing market-leading sales for the T-115.

Perhaps surprisingly, letter-reading is not yet a highly developed art in all motor companies. Senior members of the GM Design Staff told us in 1992 that they very seldom were given the opportunity to see letters from owners of the cars they designed. 'We know we receive them,' they said, 'but we aren't allowed to read them.'

BEING CUSTOMER-DRIVEN
DEMANDS A SEA-CHANGE IN ATTITUDE

During the 1980s Ford successfully changed its ideas about the role of the customer in new-car R&D activity when it launched its Taurus programme. The process required agonizing changes in executive attitudes, however. These were described to Eric Taub by Ray Ablondi, then Ford's North American director of marketing research.

Don Petersen, said Ablondi, wanted his help in advancing his 'customer-driven ideas'. 'That was a huge decision for an autocratic company like us,' Ablondi said [20]. 'To be customer-driven imposes a tremendous burden on you, because then you have to listen to what the customers want.' Based on his interviews with Ford people, Eric Taub commented further [20]:

> Listening would be a new thing for Ford management. The company had not been paying any attention to the customer. The goal

was not to give the customer what he or she wanted; it was to force-feed cars down their throats giving them what Ford management felt comfortable owning themselves as they drove to their suburban homes.

DANGER OF A TECHNO-CENTRIC MINDSET

Auto industry engineers have been in the habit, especially in Europe, of making decisions for the customer. This is not necessarily bad; getting inside the skin of the customer and acting as his or her surrogate is part of the art of customer-pleasing design. But at the R&D stage this has been difficult for the more autocratic breed of engineer.

In Europe the message is being communicated and received. Said PSA's chief Jacques Calvet [23]: 'Cars are not built to please automotive engineers, even if engineers enjoy building cars. Makers constantly need to think about the expectations that cars must meet today. These expectations have changed. Cars are built for consumers, and consumers have become more and more demanding.'

Ford in America gave its engineers a 'reality check' and found them wanting. 'The Voice of the Customer and the voice of the engineer aren't necessarily the same,' Bob Marshall of Ford told Lindsay Brooke [6]: 'We did some driveability correlations between how the customer sees driveability and how engineers evaluate it. Our engineers evaluated it somewhat differently.'

Marshall told Brooke that engineers tend to get 'mentally corrupted' by whether they think a particular solution will be accepted by management as workable. 'If you start saying, "to hell with what's practical – here's what the customer says is a problem," they take a different attitude about spending money,' Marshall said.

KEEPING AN OPEN MIND IS ESSENTIAL

If you're trying to listen to the radio and you can't hear well because there's too much static, you won't be able to get the message. The message from the customer may have to be shouted (and most customer messages are whispered) if the in-house static is too great.

Glenn Gardner, General Manager of Chrysler's Large Car Platform Engineering and former Programme Manager for the Minivan, told Gerry Kobe how important it is to keep down the background noise that interferes with good decision making [24]: 'We came close to perfection on the minivan because we didn't try to influence anything – we just learned.

'Now look at what Ford and GM did and you can see they didn't let the information they gained enlighten them enough to do the right thing,' Gardner added. 'I could almost guarantee you that if Chrysler had had a small pick-up truck at the time, with small engines, small axles and small transmissions already tooled, we might have made the same mistake. GM and Ford benchmarked the segment, but they had decided on their answers before they asked their questions.'

DISCOVER LESSONS BOTH OUTSIDE AND INSIDE

Perhaps deservedly, the motor industry has a reputation for being resistant to outside initiatives. In an interview with *Ward's Auto World* GM Executive Vice President William Hoglund revealed some of his frustrations with his system's failure to respond.

Mr Hoglund was among the first in the USA to realize that W Edwards Deming was the adviser behind many of the productivity successes enjoyed by the Japanese motor industry. Mr Hoglund suggested to his GM colleagues that they invite Mr Deming in for a meeting. The reply he received was the dismissive, 'What the hell can he teach us?'

'So what's your response?' asked Mr Hoglund. 'It's to shut up and not come up with any other stupid ideas.'

Even within GM Mr Hoglund found that his company was reluctant to draw productive lessons from new and unusual initiatives. Only very belatedly did GM learn the importance of organizational rather than automated advances to gain better productivity as demonstrated by its joint venture in California with Toyota, NUMMI.

Similarly GM's new Saturn Corporation innovated dramatically in customer-responsive marketing in its structure and dealerships after extensive research. However, said Mr Hoglund, Saturn's ideas and innovations 'were not particularly understood or desired or asked for' at the top levels of General Motors.

IMPORTANCE OF THE 'NOODLE FACTOR'

Through focus groups, direct observation, active discussion, encouragement of new ideas and the intervention of a consumer ombudsman Ford's 'Team Taurus' was able to move ahead of the status quo and design a new kind of car for Ford and Mercury. No good ideas were to be rejected, the team leader told his troops [25]:

> I want the best of everything. I don't care where it comes from. If the best ashtray is in a Honda Civic, then I want to know about it. If you are going to work for me, I expect you to try to reach perfection. You will find out that I have got a passion for perfection. There is no point in trying to reach for mediocrity, because then you will just fall short of mediocrity. And don't tell me you can't do something. Everything is possible. Just figure out a way to do it. On this project, you will be doing some pretty common things. But our success will come only if you do those common things uncommonly well.

The intent of the Taurus development team was to enhance what David E. Davis, Jr of *Automobile Magazine* calls the 'noodle factor'. This is the willingness and ability of the engineers to 'noodle' with care every feature of the design.

Less elegantly, it means that the creators of a vehicle have the patience and the concern for the customer to 'sweat the details' of a new design by taking the time and trouble to examine, check and improve every aspect of it inside and out with reference to both appearance and driver/owner satisfaction.

THOUGHTFUL DETAILS COMMUNICATE EXCELLENCE

Car makers have the power – if they choose to use it – to benefit the customer in profoundly pleasing ways. 'Properly directed economy of planning allows us today to design a car in which a person no longer feels like a fixture but perceives that everything has been conceived to meet his requirements in terms of function, psychology and taste,' said former Fiat chief designer Mario Maioli [26].

In the Ford Taurus and Mercury Sable, wrote Eric Taub [20], research showed that people appreciated their detail features 'such as a dual sun visor, power window switches angled toward the driver, a cup holder, minor but thoughtful items whose collective value was greater than the sum of their parts. The hoped-for implication was that if Ford paid so much attention to these items, they must have put out even more energy for the components that really counted.'

Ford's example was not overlooked by the designers of the new Chrysler LH models. Especially in their interiors they exhibit a very high 'noodle factor'. In every detail the cars communicate to the customer the care and concern of the people who designed them. This represents a handbrake turn in Chrysler's approach to auto design.

CUSTOMER-DRIVEN PRODUCT DEVELOPMENT:
LIGHT DAWNS AT GM

Later than Ford and Chrysler, GM has discovered the importance of really listening to the customer. Senior GM executive William Hoglund admitted to *Automotive News* that this was not a GM strength in recent years [27]: 'Alfred Sloan said, "a car for every purse and purpose." We momentarily lost sight of that.'

'A customer focus makes a big difference in how GM develops a car,' *Automotive News* quoted Arvin Mueller, Vice President and General Manager of Engineering and Design Operations since October 1992 [27]. 'In the past, GM competed by mimicking or improving on a successful competitor's product. Now, GM will let customer needs in that segment dictate the product,' Mueller said.

'The whole business, not just the marketing, now begins and ends with the customer,' said GM's Vince Barabba, executive in charge of the Marketing Research Decision Centre and Corporate Information Management. GM president Jack Smith has put his shoulder to the wheel: 'The vision is Total Customer Satisfaction,' he told reporters before the 1992 New York Auto Show. 'If you apply that to what you are doing every day, it makes you stop and think if what you're doing is in line with the vision.'

VITAL TO PUT NEW INSIGHTS AND FINDINGS TO USE

The worst crime in the car industry is to obtain good information and then fail to act upon it! Robert Shook quoted the president of Honda North America as demonstrating that [21]:

> the proof is in the actions: 'When we introduced the second-generation Prelude, we didn't put power steering in it. Women drivers complained the steering was too heavy and within six months' time we put in power steering. We react fast that way.' A fast reaction. That's part of the Honda legend.
>
> Contrast this with a story that a GM executive told *Forbes* a while back. When he wanted a pin-stripe put on his California-bound cars, production said it would take a year to get it.

This would not have surprised Alex Mair, who once headed Chevrolet Engineering and GM's Technical Staffs [28]:

> The reason the auto makers can't be as fast as they were in the past is that they have too many people not involved in designing and building cars. Plus, they have too many meetings and presentations. Why, when I started at General Motors, the only place you were allowed to meet was in the halls! And when Ed Cole was at Chevrolet, he had them re-engineer the escalators so they would go faster.

STREAMLINED MODEL RANGES
HELP THE ENTIRE SYSTEM

Earlier we mentioned the wide ranges of cars that the major producers are offering. Can they afford the time and effort needed to design all the body styles in all the ranges with an adequate 'noodle factor' – bearing in mind that nothing less is good enough in today's marketplace? The major makers are trying to reduce the model proliferation that has added greatly to their R&D burden.

Significantly, in the USA Jack Smith has declared that the General Motors product range must be pruned ruthlessly so that the company's roots may recover. *Automotive News* reports: 'Smith mandated that the new GM attend only to core products that have the potential of leading their class in sales while delivering the best customer attributes, quality and features.'

FORD'S FOCUS ON KEY MODELS AND SEGMENTS

Also in the USA, Ford has made significant progress in simplifying its model range offerings. With each new launch it has reduced the number of models and variants it produces. For example there are now only two basic Thunderbirds and four Probe models. Within each range there are a limited number of trim and value packages.

Ford dealers report that this simplified range is easier to deal with in all respects. It is easier to order cars, easier to sell them and easier to arrange their financing. Both the salesperson and the customer are less confused by excessive range variety. At Ford's end, of course, such simplification helps improve production efficiency and reduce manufacturing cost.

The Ford policy had another origin as well: a determination to build cars that appealed strongly to particular owner groups, rather than blandly to undifferentiated groups. Ray Ablondi of Ford described the logic to Eric Taub [20]:

> In 1979 Petersen and I thought 'why not try to appeal to a different market? Wouldn't we be better off, since we only have 16% of the market, that we appeal to 33% of the market, and the other 66% don't like us at all?' *Didn't like you at all*. That was the key. So when you go out and do customer research, I'll listen only to the people whom I am aiming for, and I am not going to pay attention to anybody else.

Lou Ross, in charge of R&D at Ford, was aware that this would be different to Ford's former policy of trying to appeal to everybody and offend nobody. 'But I want to go after that 25% of the market-place that would like this kind of car, those that would rate it 8 to 10, not the 40% that would hate the car or just tolerate it,' Ross said. This line of thinking led to the launch of the Taurus and Sable, cars that many credit with saving the Ford Motor Company.

MANY AUTO R&D PEOPLE ARE TOO REMOTE FROM CUSTOMERS

What other avenues are open to help senior managers in auto companies keep in touch with the needs of their customers? One attractive new idea is the 'owners' council'. We are familiar with dealers' councils, in which groups of dealers meet with their car makers from time to time to discuss issues affecting their peers. On the same principle, Audi in the USA has an owners' council.

Audi, struggling to regain a good reputation in America after its unintended acceleration problems, established an owners' council to close the gap between its customers and its management. It rotates the membership from time to time to reflect different categories and types of Audi owners. The owners' council meetings serve as sounding boards for opinions and attitudes that can be of great value to Audi's marketers and product planners.

In addition, MIT researchers hinted that it would be no bad thing if car industry executives were more personally involved in car purchase and ownership [19]:

> It is sobering to remember that no one employed by a car company has to buy a car from the dealer (they buy in-house through the company instead or even receive a free car as part of their remuneration package). Thus, they have no direct link to either the buying experience or the customer.

That things are different in Japan in this case, as in many others, is shown by an interview with Akira Uchida of Mazda, responsible for the coordination of the company's design centres in Hiroshima, Tokyo, Los Angeles and Frankfurt [29]:

> Interviewer: The car that your company makes available to you – which particular model do you like to drive?
>
> Uchida: A company car? In our company no one has such a vehicle.
>
> Interviewer: But you as a Director . . .
>
> Uchida: No one, not even the Directors. Everyone must buy his own car.

CHAUFFEUR-DRIVEN CARS REFLECT – OR SHOULD – A BYGONE ERA

Many senior car executives in Europe do not even drive their cars. They are assigned chauffeur-driven cars that emphasize a traditional industry hierarchy. 'I put a stop to that when I arrived,' said Jacques Nasser, Chairman of Ford of Europe in 1993–4 [30]. 'As I see it we're a car company and we ought to be driving our products and those of our rivals, so I eliminated the assigned cars.'

'It didn't make me very popular,' Nasser added. Perhaps not, but popularity won't win the coming battle for the consumer. Only profound product knowledge, gathered by open minds at the R&D stage, will contribute to inventing cars today that meet tomorrow's market needs and desires.

POINTS FOR DISCUSSION AND REVIEW

- Name and discuss some ways of innovating to meet the needs of a market that 'isn't there'.
- How would you define the term 'chartbuster'?
- What role can dealers play at the research and development phase of car creation?
- Give some examples from your experience of ways to carry out new-product research personally.
- Why is it very difficult for car makers to listen to the customer at the R&D phase of a new project?
- What causes engineers to be 'mentally corrupted' when evaluating new design concepts?
- What is meant by the 'noodle factor' and why is it important?

4 Customer-driven car design

How and why are new ideas in car design implemented? How should the process of designing and engineering cars in detail best take into account the needs of the consumer? Who represents the consumer in enlightened motor companies through the entire design process of bringing a car to market? These are some of the themes of this chapter, taking in the design disciplines of both styling and product engineering.

The power and importance of car design were emphasized by the findings of a 1993 J.D. Power Customer Satisfaction Study. Asked why they changed marques when they bought a new car, Americans interviewed said that their main reason was to 'try a different style'. Thus the power of a change of style is of tremendous importance as an attraction of car buyers to the marketplace.

Design's strong significance helps explain why, in the same survey, 96% of Toyota owners said they were satisfied with their car but only 87% said that they would be loyal to Toyota when they next bought a car. The availability of an attractive new design is thus a major factor in inducing customers to change marques. It also can be and is used to encourage a customer to return to a dealer to buy a new car of the same marque.

THE CHANGING MISSION OF MOTOR INDUSTRY DESIGN

Throughout 1992 Mario Maioli was responsible for all design activities in the Fiat Auto Group. From this perspective he formed an all-embracing view of the role of design in the car industry [26]:

> Design may be considered [a part of] every product whose conception, production and distribution demand the investment of a large amount of capital. Capital spending need not necessarily go on production equipment. It may be required by product conception, prototype construction, communication, marketing, after-sales service etc. The complex areas which must be carefully looked at – disregarding, for brevity's sake, all the many others – are: satisfying real needs, economy of design, technological consistency and quality levels.

But Maioli is concerned that design is not adequately meeting its responsibilities as a solver of real problems, also in the motor industry: 'Collaboration between industry and design has degenerated into a relationship that is far too cosy. Design has repudiated its rigorous planning methods for stylistic involutions on products suitable for consumer manipulation but not always consistent with the real needs and problems of society.'

Instead of superficiality, argues Maioli, design must contribute more fundamentally to the needs of humanity: 'Design must appear today in a different situation, conscious of its extended social role. The planning/production/technological context will have to be consistent not only with corporate objectives but also with social ones.' Design has great power to innovate and integrate. In Maioli's view the motor industry must exploit that power to help it meet its social obligations.

ENVIRONMENTAL EXCELLENCE IS OF OBVIOUS CUSTOMER IMPORTANCE

The environmental imperative needs to be taken on board as 'business as usual' by auto designers. They will have to respond not only to legislation but also to the heartfelt desires of their customers. Tamotsu Inagaki put it well [31]: 'As members of society, corporations cannot act in ways which defy the values of society. Consumers have developed an attitude of taking care of products and the Earth and there is a demand for products conforming to this attitude.'

The consumer must have confidence in the car maker's determination and ability to offer him or her the best environmental and occupant safety that is available in the product class. Indeed, this must be the guideline for each designer: 'My family will be driving and riding in this car. I know that cars have accidents. How well would I like them to be protected from harm? How much should this car burden their environment?'

Car manufacturers must master the pattern of potential future environmentally-led changes in consumer choice. Marketplace disruption could be provoked by tax levies according to individual national political inclinations. This should be a serious concern for all European car suppliers and especially for the 'Little Seven' manufacturers.

LIGHT WEIGHT FOR HIGH FUEL ECONOMY A CLEAR PRIORITY

If 'greenhouse gas' taxes on fuels are adopted by the Member States of the European Union, car operating costs will increase. Fuel alone would then become the most important cost component through the life cycle of a car. This would have serious consequences for the products, sales mixes, prices and not least the profits of the suppliers.

There is only one customer-friendly solution to the fuel consumption problem: the one in which the car makers secure better fuel economy through light weight and fuel-efficient engines – and thus avoid coercive taxation. Fundamental improvements in car operating characteristics would also lift from industry and commerce in general the burden of tax-led fuel cost increases and their inflationary consequences.

VIEW THE PRODUCT
AS PART OF A TOTAL QUALITY SYSTEM

Embracing all functional aspects of the car, as well as its environmental impacts, designers must think of the product in the long term, as part of a total system of service and use. 'The cost to replace a defective item on the production line is fairly easy to estimate,' said W. Edwards Deming [14], 'but the cost of the defective item that goes out to a customer defies measure.' Deming advises further:

> Neither the building of a product nor tests thereof in the laboratory and on the proving ground are sufficient to describe its quality or how it will perform or be accepted. Quality must be measured by the interaction of three participants:
> 1. the product itself;
> 2. the user and how he uses the product, how he installs it, how he takes care of it, what he was led (by advertising) to expect;
> 3. instructions for use, training of the customer and training of repairman, service provided for repairs, availability of parts.

At the design stage all partners in the creation of a car must achieve a balance of their interests if inherent quality is to be achieved. This was not always so at General Motors, said one of its engineers [22]: 'For the past several years we have struggled with a styling department that was above compromise. Never mind that it's impossible to build. The stylists cannot be questioned.' Design must lead – but it cannot domineer.

EMPLOYEE CREATIVITY MUST BE FULLY EXPLOITED

While the product is being designed and engineered, who will sit at the shoulders of the designers to guide their pens and mice on the CAD screen? Consumers can't always be present. Who is their surrogate in the design office and the factory? Professor of Management Hermann Simon has a simple answer [32]: 'In the heads of the employees sleeps the largest unused reserve of productivity, a gold mine in which hundreds, indeed thousands of ideas and opportunities for saving lie hidden.'

Professor Simon quotes the research findings of the Institute of the German Economy on the productivity of ideas, a comparison made between Japan and Germany. Studying the numbers of suggestions made by Japanese and German employees and the success of these, Professor Simon calculated an advantage of 514 times better performance in Japan than in Germany. 'To be sure,' he said, 'each German suggestion brings a larger saving, but this cannot balance out the gigantic disadvantage in the sheer quantity of successful suggestions.'

In net savings, Professor Simon found that the Japanese outperformed the Germans by a factor of 28 times. Per worker and per year a saving of DM 582 was achieved in Japan, against DM 298 in Germany. Scaled against the size of a company like Siemens with around 100 000 workers, the difference could amount to a saving of DM 2.2 billion per year.

Relating this to an assumed cost per worker of DM 100 000, Professor Simon calculated an annual productivity improvement for the Japanese of 5.9% against 0.2% for Germany: 'Perhaps we now better understand where the often-quoted productivity-improvement objectives of the Japanese companies of 6% per year have their origins.'

Professor Simon attributed a large share of the Japanese advantage to the *kaizen* concept, which 'expects of every worker that he considers every problem at all times and brings forward recommendations for improvement. Behind that stands the basic conviction that every process and every product can always be improved.'

AUTO INDUSTRY EMPLOYEES UNIQUELY ABLE TO CONTRIBUTE

These findings have powerful implications for Europe's auto industry. Many of the employees of ICI or Siemens, for example, must be designing and making products which they could and would never use in their daily lives. Their professional capability allows them to suggest better engineering or production methods, but they are never able to make recommendations for improvement of product function or service from the perspective of a customer.

The same can emphatically not be said about the auto industry. Isn't everyone an expert on cars? Have you, as a member of the industry, ever been in any social gathering at which those present did not have quite strong views about automobiles, their design and respective value? Since most people drive cars or ride in them, they have plenty of opinions about them.

No other industry making complex products has a pool of knowledge and interest in the entire workforce greater than that in the car industry. Every single person working in the car business brings with him or her their tremendous experience of the product they are making or selling, its good and bad points and its problems. Not to take full advantage of this phenomenal knowledge base would be negligence of the first magnitude.

The challenge to take advantage of this knowledge base is all the greater in the USA, where all auto workers are also drivers. The situation is different to that in Germany in the 1950s when most car workers cycled or rode streetcars to work. In those days it was necessary to organize drives and rides in the cars being built so that the workforce would better understand the nature of the products they were building. That this is no longer necessary is as obvious as the acres of parking space next to every factory.

DESIGNERS CAN BE DEMOGRAPHICALLY MATCHED TO CUSTOMERS

How, in human terms, can car makers best identify with the needs of customers at the design stage? One hint comes from Honda. Its designers work in special teams devoted to particular Honda models. In a subtle touch, Honda takes care to correlate the age of the car designers in each group to the age of the intended market for the car they are creating.

The young Honda designers start by working on the cars intended for the youngest markets. As they grow older they move over to other teams that are designing Hondas to suit older age groups. This must be a remarkably effective way of helping ensure that Hondas well suit the age groups for which they are intended.

PERSONAL INVOLVEMENT AND COMMITMENT BY DESIGNERS NEEDED

As at the R&D stage, so too at the design stage of auto development the personal involvement of the designer in the needs of the customer must be assured. Inagaki of *Car Styling* says [31]:

> It is essential to develop the attitude of continually revising the product through a process of trial and error, considering what types of problems arise when the product is actually used, whether or not there are any aspects of the product which make it difficult to use, and whether or not there are any things which cause unnecessary worry or confusion for users. To do this it is necessary to listen to the opinions of many users *and for the designers themselves to gather these opinions* [emphasis added].

Easy to say but difficult to do. Mr Inagaki adds: 'These points seem obvious, but in reality are extremely difficult to put into practice. Companies must truly understand the necessity of spending time and money to solve these problems.'

PROJECT LEADER ROLE CAN BE DECISIVE

Evidence is strong that the role of the individual, once so blithely repudiated in corporate life, is of vital importance to the success of a new car. From Europe as well as Japan and the USA comes confirmation that the role of a powerful project leader can make all the difference.

In *The Machine that Changed the World* [19] the MIT researchers discussed their findings:

> The lean producers invariably employ some variant of the *shusa* system pioneered by Toyota (termed the 'large-project leader' or LPL system at Honda). The *shusa* is simply the boss, the leader of the team whose job it is to design and engineer a new product and get it fully into production.
>
> In the best Japanese companies the position of *shusa* carries great power and is, perhaps, the most coveted in the company. For those who truly love to make things, the job brings extraordinary satisfaction. In fact, it is the best position in the modern world from which to orchestrate all the skills needed to make a wonderfully complex manufactured product, such as the automobile, come into being.

SUCCESSFUL FORD AND GM PROJECT LEADERS

In the USA, Ford's Lew Veraldi had the powers of a *shusa* when he led the team developing the Taurus/Sable. Previously he played a similar role in leading the development of the Fiesta in Europe for Ford. His strength of purpose and focus made the resulting cars much better-integrated vehicles than they might have been otherwise.

Lew Veraldi had the strong backing of Ford's chief, Don Petersen. 'With the Team Taurus project,' Petersen wrote, 'we made a point of

Fig. 4.1 The presence of a powerful yet responsive and motivating team leader or *shusa* in Lew Veraldi ensured the integrity of the creation of the Ford Taurus and Mercury Sable.

Fig. 4.2 Zora Arkus-Duntov, here behind the wheel of a 1955 test 'mule', devoted much of a long career to Chevrolet's Corvette and, by defending it, assured its survival.

Fig. 4.3 Unlike the Corvette, Ford's two-passenger Thunderbird had no strong defender. In fact before it was launched the four-passenger T-Bird was already being designed.

not passing the baton from one person to the next as we'd have done in the past. The heart of Lew Veraldi's team stayed with the Taurus programme from beginning to end.'

Referring to rival company GM, Don Petersen gave another example of the power of the personal approach to car design [17]:

I believe the reason General Motors has a Corvette today is that
one man, Zora Duntov, made that car his mission in life. Both
Ford and GM started making sports cars in the mid-1950s, GM
with its '54 Corvette and Ford with the '55 two-seater Thunderbird.
The Corvette wasn't much of a sports car at first and neither was
our Thunderbird. Ford always had some new leader stepping in,
along with whatever engineers happened to be available, but
Duntov was there with the Corvette through thick and thin.

That's how you develop a product with identity and character.
Others may have influenced the Taurus project, but Lew and his
original team stuck with his vision, providing the continuity needed
to avoid developing a mediocre car.

IMPORTANT INDIVIDUAL CONTRIBUTIONS
IN EUROPE

At European car makers the individual has often made a substantial
difference. At Fiat, wrote Dante Giacosa, Carlo Salamano, in his role
as head of vehicle testing, was for years the technical conscience of
the company [33]: 'Carlo Salamano was an important and representative character. He considered himself the first champion of Fiat's technical prestige. He never permitted doubts of his judgment because it
was the judgment of Fiat itself.'

Fig. 4.4 So influential was Fiat chief tester Carlo Salamano (here demonstrating the then-new 600) that he was regarded as the 'conscience' of the
Fiat automobile company.

Dante Giacosa wrote vividly of the characteristic way in which Salamano attacked his work:

> His wrists of steel, the quickness of his reflexes, his outstanding skill as a driver, courage and above all his invincible tenacity in getting right to the bottom of things – whether he was investigating steering, cornering, the vehicle's behaviour when it was made to veer sharply out of control, brakes, suspension, noise levels, the response of the engine in the most unpredictable situations – had all become a legend even among his fellow workers and subordinates.

Fiats, Giacosa said of Salamano, 'reflected his personality as if they were children whom he had brought up so that they absorbed his character, the good and the bad in it: basically sturdy and great-hearted even if lacking in refinement. In fact he never bothered much about appearances, especially the inside of the automobile. Safety and functional qualities were his main concern.'

Renault's new Twingo has won wide praise for its efficiency, individuality and originality. It too had the benefit of a strongly-supported project leader, Elizabeth Bougis. Ms Bougis reported that Renault's president at the time, Raymond Levy, placed full confidence in her team and gave them a free hand in developing the Twingo.

Was the selection of a woman as project leader significant? It was clear from the research into the Twingo's potential market that around half of its purchasers would be women. Certainly in these circumstances it was advantageous to have a woman in charge of the vehicle's development.

Fig. 4.5 Offering a strong appeal to female buyers, the Renault Twingo benefited from having a woman as project leader.

EXTENT OF *SHUSA* POWER UNDER CONSTANT REVIEW

How much authority should such project-leading *shusa*s be given? The worst situation arises when they haven't enough. 'In Western teams,' said the authors of *The Machine That Changed the World*, such a team leader 'is more properly called a co-ordinator, whose job it is to convince team members to co-operate. It is a frustrating role, because the leader really has limited authority, so few team leaders report enjoying it. Indeed, many company executives view the job as a dead end in which success leads to little reward and failure is highly visible.' The MIT authors added [19]:

> What's more, the team leader is in an extremely weak position to champion a project within the company. It is common in Detroit, Wolfsburg and Paris for top management to over-ride the team leader about the specifications and feel of the product – often repeatedly during the course of development. In the worst case – and all too frequently, particularly in the United States – the result is a product with no personality or distinction so the company must sell solely on the basis of low price.

In firms like Toyota, team leaders have often been granted immense powers to implement special designs for all elements of the vehicle. In a more straitened era, however, Toyota has been one of the first to review this policy for the development of its 26 product lines – the most of any maker in the world.

'Toyota is not only gradually reducing the number of model variants it makes but also reorganising its product-development setup to operate more efficiently,' Alex Taylor reported in *Fortune* [34]. 'Toyota has bunched all its vehicles into three basic groups – front-wheel drive, rear-wheel drive and trucks – and put each group under the control of a chief engineer. His goal is to make the *shusa*s cooperate with each other in order to reduce the number of unique parts by 30%.'

MANY COMPANY ACTIVITY AREAS MUST FEEL INVOLVED

More customer representation at the design stage is achieved when more of the company's disciplines are able to make a contribution. 'Unlike many auto makers that depend strictly on design engineers to develop cars,' Robert Shook wrote [21], 'Honda relies on a programme called Sales, Engineering, Design or SED. People from Sales, Engineering and R&D meet regularly from beginning to end of the project. This leads to a flow of steady ideas from which Honda can build the cars the customers want.'

At Chrysler the concept of 'ownership' of the car and its components is given heavy emphasis in product engineering. 'Ownership is still the most powerful motivator for any of us,' said Glenn Gardner, head of engineering platforms and general manager of engineering of Chrysler's well-received LH products.

According to Patrick Bedard [35], 'ownership Chrysler-style means that management doesn't tell the engineers how to design a car. It tells them what customers they have to please, how much money they have to work with and when they have to be finished, but it's up to the people working on the parts to decide how they should be.'

And in an auto company if you are not working on product development you should be aware that you may be expendable. MIT's James Womack stresses the need to focus work with laser intensity and avoid false starts and duplication of effort:

> In most Western companies, much activity is unfocused. Product planners work on products that never get the green light; massive amounts of staff waste time fighting fires. The best Japanese companies, by contrast, believe strongly that if you aren't working directly on a product actually heading for the market, you aren't adding value. So involving as many employees as possible in development work and production is vital. Companies should keep their eyes on the product the consumer will buy.

DESIGNERS CAN HAVE KEY INTEGRATING ROLE

'Industrial design's ability to integrate information from functional experts and outside partners such as distributors makes it the glue that can hold teams together and give them direction,' wrote Bruce Nussbaum in *Business Week* [18]. 'Whether they are viewed as cool professionals or wacky artistic types, designers are a key creative resource in every auto company. Their talents should be allowed to help integrate product development teams.

'As organizations de-construct themselves into "virtual corporations" made up of autonomous in-house units and various external partners, the old headquarters bureaucracies are disappearing,' Nussbaum continued in his review of 'hot products' and the designers who created them. Designers provide the vital links between and among these groups. They also add value through their direct contacts with the consumer. Nussbaum again:

> Unlike marketing, which focuses on statistical surveys to gauge attitudes and feelings, industrial design has traditionally taken an anthropological approach. Ethnographic tools, such as videotaping human behaviour and observing the work environment, are the perfect vectors for connecting companies to their customers. 'Industrial design understands the needs of the customer and knits the customer into the fabric of our product development,' says Seth Banks, Manager of Market Communications and Industrial Design and GE Medical Systems.

NEW WAYS OF THINKING
MUST GUIDE FUTURE DESIGN TEAMS

We have to set aside old compartmentalized ways of thinking as designers and managers if we are to meet the coming product needs, argues Tamotsu Inagaki in *Car Styling* [31]:

> The ideal product must have design which users do not grow tired of. Designs of current products which rely on trends and uniqueness are wearisome and will soon be a thing of the past. It is necessary to predict new technologies over the next 10 or 20 years and carefully study what new functions the product will require and how to add them to the original product. These studies must be done with the concentrated knowledge of all areas, from technology and marketing to design, manufacture and sales.

The way we now organize ourselves may be neither creative nor responsive enough to meet this challenge, Inagaki adds: 'Conferences held in the way that they are today will definitely not provide the right answers. It will likely be necessary to start by re-thinking the idea of the conference room itself.'

EARLY COMMITMENT TO PROJECT AIMS IS NEEDED

According to the MIT studies, Harvard researchers Clark and Fujimoto 'found that many Western development efforts fail to resolve critical design trade-offs until very late in the project.' This often means that customer-pleasing features, agreed for inclusion at the outset, have to be modified or abandoned as the project nears its end. And without such features, no car can successfully combine volume with profitability.

Why does this occur? Womack, Jones and Roos say the reason is that no real commitment to the ultimate aims is made [19]:

> U.S. team members show great reluctance to confront conflicts directly. They make vague commitments to a set of design decisions – agreeing, that is, to try to do something, so long as no reason crops up not to. In Japan, by contrast, team members sign formal pledges to do exactly what everyone has agreed upon as a group. So conflicts about resources and priorities occur at the beginning rather than at the end of the process.

The management process known as QFD (quality function deployment) is designed to overcome this reluctance to commit. To use QFD, all team members must consider the needs of the customer and then the product at the outset, before actual design work starts. Although considered by many to be too cumbersome to justify wide use in the car industry, QFD as a discipline has the merit of stressing an early decision and a sense of unity among design team members.

CHARACTER CANNOT BE OUTSOURCED

Designers can work effectively both inside and outside companies. But strong, dedicated work by a core in-house design team is essential to the creation of a car with the intense and individual personality that has strong customer appeal, Alex Mair believes [28]:

> Once you move outside with many businesses doing your engineering, it begins to level off the differentials that separate one car from another. The more fragmented the designs of all these components becomes, the less character a car will have. And it's the cars that have the most character that are the best in the long run.
>
> Look at how good Honda's shift effort is. They didn't just design a good shift lever. They designed the whole power train as a package. You can't buy an engine from one company, a transmission from another and a clutch from another and get that shift effort.

SHARED VEHICLES POSE NEW CHALLENGES

Car makers are being challenged afresh to master all aspects of design in detail in the new era in which products are shared between manufacturers. An example in the USA is Honda's 4×4 Passport sport-utility, which was first marketed from December 1993. The Passport is not made by Honda but in fact is an Isuzu Rodeo, built in Lafayette, Indiana.

A few cosmetic changes separate the Passport from the Rodeo. But one area that the designers failed to touch was the engine room. As a result, when a potential Passport buyer in a Honda showroom looked under the hood and saw 'Isuzu' on the engine he put aside the nearly-completed sales agreement and left the dealership.

Fig. 4.6 Apart from minor cosmetic and identity differences the Isuzu-built Rodeo (left) and the Isuzu-built Honda Passport (right) are identical. Such sharing of models between brands creates new tensions in the marketplace.

Fig. 4.7 General Motors faced a daunting challenge in the restyling of its German-built Omega (Vauxhall version shown at left) to constitute a valid Cadillac-brand entry. The Cadillac Catera was foreshadowed by the LSE concept car (right).

The customer had come in because he was a loyal Honda buyer who wanted a 4×4, but he wanted it to be Honda through and through. The lesson? If Honda considered it fair to put its nameplate and emblems on the vehicle it should have done the same with the engine.

Within motor companies, designers have long had to create marque distinctiveness while making single models serve several dealer bodies. Recently, however, such actions are international in scope. One of the most ambitious such projects is GM's launch in America of the Cadillac Catera version of the Opel Omega in 1996. Cadillac needs a new model to appeal to more youthful buyers; the Omega built in Germany has the right credentials in terms of technology and size to meet this requirement.

But can a car conceived and designed to be successful in Europe as a top-range Opel also be successful in the USA as an entry-level Cadillac? The answer is that it will only be successful if the designers of the Opel-based Cadillac Catera were given enough freedom and enough budget to alter the car's design to make it a convincing Cadillac. It is no small challenge.

POINTS FOR DISCUSSION AND REVIEW

- What evidence is there that Japanese companies are particularly productive in generating new ideas?
- What special attribute gives the auto industry an advantage over all other business in generating customer-pleasing design ideas?
- Discuss the advantages and disadvantages of having strong leaders for new projects.
- Why does the role of the designer become even more important when car companies reorganize?
- Name and discuss examples of sharing of similar products between companies and brand names.
- What does Chrysler mean by 'ownership' of a car or component?

Customer-driven car production 5

It would be a rare car owner who has ever seen a car factory, and vice versa. The hectic and hazardous activity of the factory floor is not the place for hordes of customers. But the customer must be present in the workplace. How is this to be achieved? We address and answer this key question in this chapter.

HIGH MANUFACTURING QUALITY IS ESSENTIAL – BUT...

Can any guide to the customerization of manufacturing suggest that the products leaving the plant can be anything but perfect? Ordinarily not. But the introduction of the original Ford Taurus was the exception that proved the rule.

The Taurus was launched at a quality level poorer than its predecessor. A rare completely-new car, it had more than the normal complement of faults. Nevertheless, wrote Lindsay Brooke [6], 'in the Taurus's first eighteen months of production, the car's fresh styling and new image offset many early problems that may have sunk other cars.'

Bob Marshall, in charge of quality for Ford, pointed out that quality is a process based on design, manufacturing and dealer performance. As such, he said, quality is achieved by 'increasing Things Gone Right, more than reducing Things Gone Wrong.' Said Brooke, 'Ford's success with Taurus was that in the early days they had enough Things Gone Right that they simply swamped the Things Gone Wrong – it was a very customer-driven car in its design and content.'

Thus the Taurus's customer-pleasing design and content came to the aid of the production people, giving them the time they needed to sort out the car's teething troubles. Ford's dealers also came to the party, fixing customer cars quickly. Now the Taurus is built in one of America's highest-quality and most productive facilities.

PRODUCTION AT LEAST AS IMPORTANT AS PRODUCT

In creating the Taurus, design and production people cooperated as never before at Ford. Recognition for the first time was given to the huge contribution that the manufacturing process can make to the success of a product. That ingenious and responsive manufacturing can make a core contribution to success in the marketplace is a theme developed by editor and economist Rupert Pennant-Rea [36]:

> There is no great lasting virtue now in inventing products. The advantage lies in mastering the processing of products; in making them more reliably; making them more cheaply; making them to designs that really suit customers, changing customer needs and the ability to latch on to changes in customer taste and to get the products suitable to those tastes quickly to market; and to give them all the backup that is needed for reliability and service.

While the invention itself is important, Pennant-Rea argues, it does not necessarily bring direct economic benefit to a city, county or country. The benefit comes from the ability of intelligent, confident, versatile men and women to adapt the invention to customer needs and to keep adapting it as those needs change and evolve.

EUROPEANS LAGGING
IN MANUFACTURING PRODUCTIVITY

The inherent quality, reliability, cost, value for money and prompt delivery of what the customer ultimately elects to buy are determined in the final outcome by the efficiency of the production plants and the skill with which the cars are engineered.

Experts on car production as conducted in Japan are contemptuous of the manufacturing efforts of the Europeans. Judging by the progress to date, said Kenichi Sekine in 1993 [37], 'in ten years a Japanese car will have displaced the Golf as the European market leader.'

In his reviews of German producers of various products Sekine, working for the Bossard consulting firm, found that many had not adopted even the bare essentials of lean production. Work didn't start on the dot in the morning, as it does in Japan. Too few working shifts were inadequately employing the capital equipment. Machinery was not organized to allow one worker to feed several machines, leading to excessive idle time for workers. Transport was poorly organized.

'In production,' said Sekine, 'the Germans have to fix a lot of things. With your machines and our organization and working time we would produce three times as much. We don't have 35-hour weeks and 30-day holidays – we work 50 and 60 hours if the company needs us.' Asked which was most important, a lean-production concept or training, Kenichi Sekine replied, 'In the auto industry it's 100% training.'

Fig. 5.1 Britain's Unipart is a leader among the component companies that are placing heavy emphasis on employee training. The company has established its own 'Unipart University'.

IMPLEMENTING THE BENEFITS OF TRAINING

The lessons learned from the Japanese emphasis on training have not been ignored in the West. Progressive British component supplier Unipart highlighted the problems facing the vehicle-manufacturing industry in a recent survey. Fully 80% of the young people it surveyed said that they see manufacturing as being vital to the future of the British economy. In sharp contrast, however, only 9% of them said that they would consider a career in manufacturing.

Unipart has taken steps to contribute to better understanding by establishing the 'Unipart University' or Unipart 'U'. This educational facility provides 14 lecture rooms and group working rooms in some 13 000 square feet of offices built at a cost of £2.5 million. It is large enough to accommodate about 10% of the Unipart Group's workforce, some 400 employees, at one time.

Practical courses staffed by Unipart managers offer a flexible programme highly responsive to the needs of the organization. Local community and school groups also have access to the Unipart 'U', as do the company's suppliers and customers.

Fig. 5.2 Unipart group chief executive John Neill (in shirtsleeves) is among those who have learned from a seemingly simple set of blocks at the Unipart 'U' how the *kanban* system works.

COPING WITH CURRENCY APPRECIATION

Nor are the pace-setting Japanese resting on their laurels. Car makers in countries whose currencies are appreciating in value should take note of the ways in which the Japanese motor firms have been coping with the challenge of *endaka*, the strengthening of the yen over recent years. They have cut production costs sharply in response, sometimes in unusual ways.

For example, Toyota declared Thursday and Friday to be the 'weekend' in some factories. This allowed production to continue on Saturday and Sunday, when the cost of electricity was lower.

'In addition,' reported the *International Herald Tribune* [38], 'because Japan has virtually no natural resources of its own, nearly everything that goes into a car made there has to be imported, and imports have become cheaper because of the currency changes. One analyst estimates that 20 billion to 30 billion yen of savings originated that way.' Is there a hint here of a way forward for Germany's car makers?

One German maker, BMW, has not overlooked the advantages of a shift in working hours to gain efficiency. At its Regensburg plant the BMW workers have a mid-week day off, working nine hours in the remaining four weekdays for a 36-hour total. Every three weeks, however, they also arrive at the plant at 5 a.m. on a Saturday to put in a day's work. The result: BMW can run the Regensburg line for 99 instead of 80 hours a week to gain better use of its capital equipment [39].

CONTINUOUS MANUFACTURING IMPROVEMENT IS MITSUBISHI'S AIM

At Mitsubishi the concept of *kaizen* in car manufacturing, usually interpreted as 'continuous improvement', is implemented as 'rationalization by all employees'. This theme implies that all members of the workforce are able to meet new challenges and are constantly motivated to do so as part of their job philosophy.

Mitsubishi, says the company's Yoichi Nakane, is dedicated to the elimination of *muri*, *mura* and *muda* as a means of rationalization. They mean, respectively, pushing beyond capacity, deviations in quality and the waste of resources. Any of the three can be destructive to the smooth development and improvement of production.

Eliminating *muri*, *mura* and *muda* has the further advantage that work becomes more enjoyable as well as more efficient. Also making work less unpleasant and difficult is the striving at Mitsubishi for the elimination of *kitsui* (hard work), *kitani* (dirty work) and *kiken* (dangerous work).

Mr Nakane also points out that Mitsubishi makes a quarter of the specialized robots that it needs for vehicle and body assembly. Through making its own robotic equipment, says Nakane, Mitsubishi increases its knowledge about the way such robots can and should be used.

USING VERSATILITY TO MAINTAIN MODEL VARIETY

The main thrust of Mitsubishi's efforts is to improve and increase production versatility by training its workers to have many different skills and capabilities. This gives its factories flexibility in both model changeovers and the offering of wide ranges of equipment and body styles.

So flexibly are they trained that each worker is able to change his job every two hours in Mitsubishi's Japanese plant. Says Mr Nakane, this is possible 'if the manager uses what is above the neck in his workers as well as what is below the neck.'

This is Mitsubishi's response to the challenge of the need for model diversity. It has no intention of slowing its 'product churning' by reducing its model ranges or the variations within them. On the contrary, its aim is to introduce more flexible automation that can respond more quickly to changes in models and designs and simple low-cost automation were needed to achieve lean production.

This thrust is especially important for Mitsubishi, which intends to match such rivals as Nissan and Toyota in model diversity. To achieve this, however, it is prepared to reduce the complexity of the components used within its vehicles. This must be and is a major design objective in support of more rational production.

RIGOROUS STANDARDS
MUST MEASURE IMPROVEMENT

Improvements in production require not slogans and generalities but specific performance measurements that can be seen and understood by the workforce, says Larry Bossidy, Chairman and CEO of global component supplier AlliedSignal. States Mr Bossidy [40]:

> Customers should be first in our minds every day and in everything we do; if we cannot satisfy them, we don't have jobs. Visit any of our plants from Sutherland to Singapore and you will find posted on our bulletin boards not slogans or motivational posters but graphs which chart the improvements wrought by one or more of our 6000 teams – or which clearly proclaim the need for improvement. AlliedSignal employees in 40 countries speak in different tongues, but they are beginning to talk the same language of the customer focus, teamwork, cycle-time reduction, speed, continuous improvement and zero-defect products.

'Customer focus' in the supplier industry can of course refer to the OEMs as well as to the end customer, the car purchaser. Increasingly car makers are asking their suppliers to help meet the quality and reliability needs of the end customer. For this reason suppliers are developing their own channels to gain intelligence about the demands of car buyers and drivers.

GREAT SUPPLIERS ARE MADE, NOT BORN

Carefully nurturing suppliers, believes Nissan in Britain, is better than the old hire-and-fire style of operation. 'We will never have the world's best car unless we have the world's best suppliers,' says Peter Hill, Purchasing Director for Nissan in Sunderland.

Because Nissan operates a single-sourcing policy, it must help its suppliers improve their performance. When some suppliers were struggling with the launch of the Primera in 1990, instead of looking elsewhere Nissan learned from the experience and helped them correct their mistakes. Peter Hill says: 'Two years later those same suppliers came in with a near-perfect launch of the Micra.'

Nissan's 197 suppliers are constantly evaluated according to a system focusing on quality, cost, delivery, development and management (QCDDM). Suppliers to Nissan in Sunderland have steadily improved their ability to deliver on time. In 1992, 84% of them were meeting a delivery date within an eight-day window. In 1993 the window shrank to three days and within it on-time deliveries were improved to 96%.

Nissan's Managing Director and CEO, Ian Gibson, had a stern warning for those who would like to match this performance [41]: 'Any company really serious about partnerships has to take a damned hard look in the mirror and change their own business internally first. You can't have a genuine two-way stream with suppliers unless you have open relationships between the functions and levels in your own business.'

THE IGNACIO LOPEZ VISION OF CUSTOMER-FOCUSED MANUFACTURING

The problems of the German auto industry and the progress made there in recent years by Opel conjoin in the personality of Ignacio 'Inaki' Lopez, the zealous and controversial industrial engineer from Spain's Basque country. Lopez has spoken often of his conviction that 'customer-focused manufacturing' is the way forward for the West's car industry.

Lopez believes that customer-focused manufacturing requires creativity, training and application, not investment in capital equipment. He is also well-known for his desire to source widely and cheaply outside the car maker's own organization. Lopez's customer focus was explained further by Al Fleming in *Automotive News* [42]:

> Lopez eschews the traditional cost–price equation in which a manufacturer determines its costs, adds a reasonable profit and sets the price. He reverses the equation. By listening to the retail customer, Lopez says, you measure market price; then you subtract the profit; then you determine the cost. You must be able to develop your products to fit the cost, he says, because 'the best way to increase profits is to reduce costs.'
>
> Lopez advocates only having value-added operations; detecting defects and eliminating the root causes; using small-lot production, just-in-time principles and one-piece flow, emphasising zero defects; having a comprehensive information system; and emphasising teamwork and good employee relations.

TEAMWORK REACHES DEEPLY INTO PRODUCTION PROCESSES

When Chrysler's new Neon small car went into production at Belvedere, Illinois in 1993, it was the first car launched by Chrysler to have been developed from the outset by an integrated platform

Fig. 5.3 For the launch of its all-important Neon model Chrysler placed heavy emphasis on training to create a strong spirit of teamwork among suppliers, engineers and factory workers.

team. The use of real teamwork throughout the process of designing and producing the Neon led to a number of unusual practices at the plant:

- Of the 3250 union workers at the plant, 1000 were flown to Chrysler's Technology Centre in Michigan to work on the cars on the pilot line there and help improve their design for manufacturing.
- The earliest vehicle in Chrysler's development series, an F1 prototype, was built by hourly workers. This gave these union men and women the chance to influence key points in the design of the car.
- When Belvedere previously built cars the plant had 600 suppliers. For Neon only 207 suppliers are delivering to the plant.
- No supplier may have more than four days of inventory at the plant.
- When production began, a representative of the supplier of fasteners to the assembly line worked for weeks next to Chrysler's employees, checking torques and improving fastening techniques.
- Twenty-six of the 100 torque-controlled tools on the assembly line are programmed to stop the line if they detect any problems with quality.
- At nearly every union work station a display shows the results of the most recent J.D. Power Initial Quality Survey. It shows the cars that the Neon will have to beat in order to get into the Top Ten models.

REWARD SYSTEMS
THAT BUILD AND STRENGTHEN TEAMWORK

The introduction of teamwork is an important trend in production at all levels, intended to make work more rewarding psychologically and thus to introduce an atmosphere in which constant improvement is a way of life. Teamwork is replacing the old lone-wolf style of manufacturing. With teams, however, the problem remains of how best to incentivize the efforts of the team members. Must the team be no stronger than its weakest link?

This problem has been tackled by Motorola in the awarding of merit pay to its shop-floor operators at its plant in Chaumberg, Illinois. Money from the merit-pay pool is first allocated to the teams, on the basis of their overall performance. Then, within the team, the team pool is allocated according to the team's assessment of the performance of each individual.

The team-member voting on the performance of the individual team members is based on performance goals set at the beginning of a production year. Achievement of these goals is measured both for the team and, by the voting within the team, for the individual members.

Motorola's experience shows that the system helps members of a work team put peer pressure on their co-workers to perform better. Since Motorola has a record of successful practices in labour-management co-operation, its 'team-based pay' programme is being closely watched by other companies.

IN CHARGE OF THE PRODUCTION LINE:
THE CUSTOMER

Implicit in the most advanced manufacturing concepts is that the customer should be in charge of the production line – not the other way around, as in the days of the sellers' market. Writing in 1941, Alfred Sloan stressed the requirement to build cars to order as much as possible [43]:

> This is the answer to a question frequently asked – Why does not General Motors make cars for stock in those periods of the year when consumer buying is at a minimum? We do in a degree. Standard combinations of colours and trim permit a floating supply in the hands of our dealers. But to sell all possible, we make cars 'to order' to please individual taste; by doing so we create additional business, even though it entails more work.

To a clear thinker like Sloan, it was obvious that only by this means would it be possible to maintain a healthy distribution system – a linkage that many of his successors have chosen to ignore. Required is production that is as responsive as possible to market demand.

Flexible production techniques, able to build the right model mix in the right quantities, are needed to avoid regular sales network disruptions and failures.

EARLY MANUFACTURING LESSONS TOO SOON FORGOTTEN

Alfred P. Sloan, Jr wrote about his experiences when leading General Motors [43]:

> Rapidly increasing volume in the prosperous days in the latter half of the 1920s served to obscure the fact that the economic strength of the retail end of the business was being sapped by the constantly increasing competition. I realised that the big problem of the product – engineering and manufacturing was becoming secondary and was being outranked by an equally big job of injecting into the distribution end of our business the scientific approach. I saw that as all cars approached a more common level of usefulness the strength of the distribution system would be the most important factor in the competitive race.
>
> Markets must be defined and protected. Enough dealers of the right size to deliver the potential of those markets and no more. Production must be determined by retail – no longer by the ambition for big figures – and statistics must be made available to chart the course. We had to get the facts and act accordingly. This we did in a very comprehensive way.

Sloan's words would speak as eloquently about the 1980s and their significance for the 1990s. 'Production must be determined by retail' – i.e. by the customer. At the end of the assembly line stands the final customer. Everything in between is expensive overhead.

POOR SPECIAL-ORDERING CAUSES CUSTOMER FRUSTRATION

In the USA cars can still be built to the customer's order, and some customers want this facility. Even more would want it if it were made more readily available to them. Through special ordering, someone who is very particular about their car can have it specified and built exactly to his or her requirements. Further, they know that a special-ordered car hasn't been languishing for months or even years waiting for a buyer.

But American dealers are unhappy that it takes as long as four to six weeks to get such a car after it is ordered. They find this a long time for customers to wait when they are very excited about having the new car they special-ordered. The car makers appear to be creating problems for themselves by permitting special orders and then not providing the cars promptly.

SPECIAL ORDERS ARE PART OF
THE PRODUCTION SYSTEM IN JAPAN

We find the Japanese car producers setting a standard in fast special-ordering, simply because it is the most efficient way to run a car company. 'From an early date Eiji Toyota and his marketing expert, Shotaro Kamiya, began to think about the length between the production system and the consumer,' wrote MIT's auto researchers [19]:

> The dealer became part of the production system as Toyota gradually stopped building cars in advance for unknown buyers and converted to a build-to-order system in which the dealer was the first stop in the *kanban* system, sending orders for pre-sold cars to the factory for delivery to specific customers in two to three weeks. To make this workable, however, the dealer had to work closely with the factory to sequence orders in the way the factory could accommodate.
>
> Since most cars are manufactured to order, there is no expanse of finished vehicles to buy off the lot and no 60- or 70-day stock of cars running up interest costs. In Japan the stock of finished cars in the system averages only 21 days (versus 66 days on average in the United States over a recent decade).

The MIT experts concluded that in Japan 'distribution is a fully integrated part of the entire production system'. They found that in the factories auto production 'is driven by the needs of the customer, not by the needs of the factory'.

Their conclusion was that 'in an increasingly competitive world market where more affluent customers are seeking – and are able to pay for – a greater choice in personal transportation, this re-orientation of the entire mass-production system will be critical for [company] survival.'

WORLDWIDE CONCENTRATION
ON FAST PRODUCT DELIVERY

Toyota's customer-driven production system can deliver to the buyer on Friday a vehicle they special-ordered the previous Monday. But this example of flexible, responsive manufacturing is by no means unique, *Fortune* reported: 'Buyers of Motorola pagers can order from a variety of features in several million combinations and have the finished product shipped to them within two hours.'

Nor are Toyota and its personnel satisfied with their accomplishments to date. They have set a domestic objective of 48 hours for delivery from order of a new automobile. As they fully integrate their manufacturing and selling systems abroad, in Europe as well as the USA, these systems too will be organized to pull cars through the plants in response to the desires of individual customers.

NEW FORECASTING RESPONSIBILITIES FOR DEALERS

The world's car makers are taking up this new challenge. In 1994 the Sales Director of Ford's British operation, Patrick Byrne, said that it was Ford's objective to produce and deliver cars to customer orders within 15 days:

> We've made a decision to do it and we are working on changing production techniques and culture, and are looking at technology and training. When the customer comes in and asks for a model with a certain colour and specification it should be available. At the moment if it's not in stock it takes anything from two to twelve weeks, or the customer has to take what's in stock.

Mr Byrne expects this fast-track production and delivery system to be up and running on at least several Ford models by 1997. As part of this new system, said Mr Byrne, there would be a greater responsibility on the part of dealers to forecast consumer trends. 'It won't be good enough for the dealers to just agree with us. They're going to have to anticipate what the customer wants more than they do now,' he added. This, he said, would be assisted by providing dealers with more advanced information about future products so that they are better placed to play their part in forecasting specific demand patterns.

COMPUTING POWER WILL COME TO THE RESCUE

Unsettling though it may be to the *status quo*, the auto industry has no choice but to make use of the new electronic technologies to make and deliver cars faster. As Bill Gates of Microsoft has put it, in a few years the real cost of computing power will be negligible.

It will cost virtually nothing to have computers available as an integral part of elements of a vehicle or vehicle system or manufacturing system. Such power will oblige auto makers to use it to find ways to build cars virtually to individual customer order in a highly efficient manner.

Such a transformation could result in dramatic changes to the way we make cars today. It will deeply influence relationships between suppliers and customers in the making and assembly of cars. Difficult though their implementation may be, the exploitation of these new methods cannot be long postponed.

TAG-READING SCANNERS
CAN HELP CONTROL PRODUCTION

An example of these techniques is the use of electronic 'tags' on cars and/or parts read by 'scanners' in the manufacturing system. The tags, which are rugged enough to withstand the knockabout of the factory floor, are computer chips which can receive, store and download large amounts of information when informed or interrogated by the radio scanners.

'In plants building Chrysler Corp's newest lines of cars and Jeeps,' wrote Al Fleming [44], 'radio frequency identification helps choreograph vehicle bodies through operations such as welding, painting and trim, then returns them to assembly-line conveyors in precise sequence to match just-in-time deliveries from suppliers. Ford Motor Co., GM and Volkswagen also use radio frequency identification to help maintain order in complex assembly operations.'

EUROPE'S AUTO INVENTORIES ARE EXCESSIVE

As in America, the level of inventory in Europe's car distribution system has scarcely changed for decades. Some of Europe's car makers still defend high stock levels for dealers. They say that customers want to see a full range of cars in dealerships and are unwilling to wait for cars built to order. They also say that high dealer stocks cover the highs and lows in demand and delivery cycles.

In fact, much of the dealer's stock is held in fields, parks or disused airfields which are quite unsuitable for customer access and inspection. In metropolitan areas, the situation is even worse. Most of the stock is held (at high cost to the dealers) in secure areas to prevent vandalism.

Thus many of the advances being made in productivity and faster reaction times to changed supply requirements, with consequent cost savings, are being squandered in excessive stocking levels for which the manufacturers are paying most of the bill. In volume franchises the manufacturers are paying for dealer stocking for up to 60 days, some even longer. New ways must be found to reduce these inventory burdens of both cost and time.

PRODUCTION MUST RESPOND TO STOCK LEVELS

Tim Rayment reports that the Japanese makers keep inventories down by shrewd production planning [45]: 'The Japanese produce 80% of their cars by assuming the market will be similar to the previous year, and make the final 20% only when they have orders. If the market drops by 10%, the cars do not get made. Europe is not as efficient because the lower cost of land means that car makers are content to stockpile stock. There is usually 60 days' supply in the system compared with 15 days in Japan.'

In addition, the multiple handling of high stock levels compromises delivered car quality. We have surveyed several markets in which up to 60% of new cars have been moved at least once from the original dealer assignment before being sold. This causes much needless vehicle aging and wear and tear.

STREAMLINED LOGISTICS NEEDED FOR CUSTOMER SATISFACTION

As a logical extension of the production line to the customer, car makers should streamline their ordering and delivery systems. European makers in particular should take advantage of the potential of their new Single Market to get ordered cars quickly from the factory to the customer in first-class condition.

It took a supplier to the industry to put this argument with convincing force. Ron Roudebush of Rockwell made his point this way [46]:

> Rockwell can build a sunroof for a car manufacturer with 136 minutes of lead time. We assemble specifically to part numbers. We bar code it. We put the vehicle identification number on it. We load it onto a cart. We drive it for twenty minutes to the customer's plant. If the supplier can provide parts to a factory to assemble cars in line sequence, 136 minutes after an order is received, why can't an OEM deliver a car to the customer in a week – instead of two to three months? Why does just-in-time stop at the OEM assembly plant?
>
> After all, most people find buying a new car to be exciting. They don't want to have to wait weeks and months to get exactly *what they want*. So, maybe the car they accept from the dealer inventory isn't just the right colour or it doesn't have power windows or whatever other options. But they take it, anyway. In essence, the car buyer still pays a lot of money to get what's merely expedience or available – not what the buyer *really* wants.
>
> It's interesting to note that foreign competition has very little success penetrating the Class 8 heavy truck market in North America. There is one major reason for this: nearly every truck is custom-designed and custom-specified for the person who wants to buy it. Think about what that would mean to the car market.
>
> Certainly, the new-car buyer would be happy. No second-choice colour, interior or options. No waiting. The OEM would be happy. No need to make cars that sell on the books but not off the lots. No second guesses. The suppliers' schedules that already change erratically every day would then change in response to the true end-user – the customer – and not to the whims of a scheduler. And the dealer would be happy too. No big inventory. No rebates, pure discounts or other gimmicks to sell cars. There would be less cost for financing, insurance and other overheads.

Physical distribution is discussed in this chapter because it is seen today as an outgrowth and extension of car manufacturing. However, we consider that the fast-response logistics systems of the future should report to the sales arm of the business rather than to manufacturing. Only by making logistics accountable to sales will its performance be measured and rewarded appropriately.

STORAGE CENTRES AND POOLS
HELP SPEED DELIVERIES

As part of its programme to speed the delivery of finished cars to customers, GM's Vauxhall introduced a system of vehicle storage centres in the UK in May 1993. Vauxhall's objective, said its Manager of Traffic Planning and Operations, Andy Mills, is 'to provide a quality product, at the right price, delivered on time. We want customers to wait no longer than seven days – or four for delivery plus two or three for dealer prep – between the time they place their order and the time they take delivery. Our vehicle storage centres are making this possible.'

Vauxhall established its vehicle storage centres at Ellesmere Port, Luton, Port Burtbury, Purfleet and Hartlepool. Instead of carrying heavy stocks at their own premises, dealers have access to a pool of products at each of the five centres. Although dealers still contribute to storage costs, these are lower at these sites by virtue of their consolidation.

The optimum lead time from order to delivery, Vauxhall has determined, is four days. By December 1993, 96.9% of orders were delivered within this time span. This represented an important step forward in achieving customer satisfaction through better logistical organization.

INCREASED SALES FORECAST
FROM FAST-RESPONSE ORDERING

In Florida another GM operation, Cadillac, is experimenting with a pooled inventory system to speed delivery of its cars to customers. In a regional distribution centre at Orlando, some 1500 popularly-equipped Cadillacs are kept in stock, about a 30-day supply. The colours and equipment of cars stored at the centre are determined by dealers, who are asked to define the most popular build combinations. They identified a mix of 250 models.

If the centre can provide a car needed by one of Cadillac's 42 dealers in Florida, the unit can be delivered in 24 hours. If a car needs to be built to a special order it will be produced on a priority basis in Michigan and delivered within two to three weeks. This is far less than the customary eight to twelve weeks needed to build and deliver a specially-ordered car.

The cars in the distribution centre are owned by the dealers, who are billed for floorplanning expenses in proportion to the cars that they draw from the centre each month. Dealers still have the same number of pre-floorplanning days and access to special offers that they had under the previous arrangement.

Cadillac estimates that the programme has the potential to increase its sales in Florida by 10 to 11 percent. The system, for which the

Florida test began in September 1994, will be introduced nationally if it proves successful.

OUTSIDE SUPPLIERS CAN MANAGE STOCK POOLS

In some situations where central stock is held to facilitate the delivery to dealers, a manufacturer engages an outside company to manage the facility. Walon, for example, is providing logistical support to the Ford/Volkswagen MPV plant in Portugal.

Walon uses a comprehensive computer system and hand-held bar-coding equipment to manage vehicle stocks, which can rise to as many as 25 000 cars on site. Individual cars can be quickly identified and delivered as required.

Walon considers that the other advantages of such central stocking systems are that less inventory overall is required to achieve fast delivery to customers. A further advantage is that inter-dealer transfers of new cars are sharply reduced. Increasing both costs and wear and tear, such transfers can take place in as many as half of dealers' new-car sales.

STEPS TOWARD CUSTOMER-PLEASING ORDERING

Kenneth Baker, Vice President of GM's Research and Development Centre, has set some of the most ambitious targets for reduction of the order-to-delivery cycle. 'I don't think it's "Star Wars" ', Baker said at the University of Michigan's Management Seminar. On Day One of Baker's cycle the buyer would select the base vehicle, specify a colour, indicate all the trim items and accessories they want – even unique seating contours – at a dealer's computerized ordering station.

When the car's build is scheduled at the factory, says Baker, orders would quickly go to component suppliers, with requests for just-in-time delivery. By the end of Day Two, the vehicle would be assembled and on its way. On Day Three the buyer would take delivery.

As an example of the possibilities, Baker points to the process used to print the upholstery of the 1993 Indy Pace car edition of Chevrolet's Camaro. This uses a computer-driven system that can start with any photo or artwork and replicate it in fabric. Any image could be used in the interior. A picture of your children on the seat back? A scenic view of your favourite river? It is easily done.

With such computerized customization, Baker believes [47], 'Our customer will define a product, right down to the fuzzy dice.' Instead of producing identical vehicles his goal is to achieve an 'economic lot size of one'.

SATISFYING CUSTOMER NEEDS
WITH 'AGILE MANUFACTURING'

The same theme was developed by Mike Mutchler, GM Vice President and Group Executive in Charge of North American Car Platforms, at an SAE meeting in 1993. With a flexible and responsive system, said Mutchler, which he called 'agile manufacturing', dealers would need to stock few vehicles apart from samples and demonstration cars.

Mutchler said [48]:

> I don't think the car dealers know how this will affect them yet, and I don't think we have the answer or the solution to that yet. But I think we are on the fringe of inventing the capability to become more agile in response to the marketplace.
>
> The reason for trying to become agile – first to understand it and then to get there – is to learn how to react fast to what that customer wants. Our dealers might become simulation centres rather than dealers as they are today.

CUSTOMER-FACING SYSTEM ELEMENTS
VERY IMPORTANT

Computer systems are being used in dealerships to help customers select particular models, colours and equipment items that they may require, as later chapters explain. But car makers have a vision that the computer will complete the transaction and send the resulting order directly to the factory for vehicle assembly. Such a procedure, being developed by Rover, is known as business process management systems (BPMS).

Based on Microsoft Windows, the custom-written BPMS programme uses sophisticated multimedia techniques to take the customer through a buying routine without the direction of a salesperson. In addition to still pictures, the system can show video demonstrations of a particular vehicle and its systems and features.

Using BPMS, developed with the help of Digital and Microsoft, customers can see the price implications of their choices and the impact it will have on their monthly payments for a selected finance plan. Before the decision is made to buy, BPMS will take into account the value of the trade-in and make a forecast of the delivery date. When the customer is satisfied, the order is transmitted to the build-line computer at the factory for the assembly of a vehicle.

Said Rover's Managing Director for Europe, 'People in the main are apprehensive that a salesman might force on them a deal that they don't want for a vehicle that they don't want. Our new systems will go a long way to removing this fear, because they provide genuinely shared information, on screen, as part of the discussion.'

IMPLICATIONS OF
BYPASSING DEALER WHEN ORDERING

A major implication of such a system would be the disregard it would show for the dealer, who is effectively bypassed by the establishing of a direct link between the customer and the car maker. This conflicts with the scenario in which the dealer is given the responsibility to help forecast future patterns of vehicle demand.

Will the information generated by such computerized ordering systems be accessible to the dealer as well? It should be, and in an organized manner, if the dealer is to be able to draw upon the trends indicated by customers at their consoles when they are considering and ordering future vehicles. Otherwise dealers will be denied the information they need to give guidance to their vehicle suppliers.

A further dimension has been added by the terms of the new Block Exemption, extending at least to 2002. This provides for the joint agreement of car makers and their dealers on sales and other key targets. In reaching such agreement, the dealers will need fully as much access to information about sales trends and demand patterns in their regions as the car makers have. Will this be provided by the vehicle supplier or will dealers have to forage for it themselves? Each auto company may approach this differently.

PILOT-TESTING OF DIRECT ORDERING BY VOLVO

In 1993 Volvo announced the pilot-testing of a new car ordering system that will give (or appear to give) the customer direct access to the manufacturing process. Three British dealerships were the first to be equipped with the new system, which is intended to be rolled out to all dealers in the UK and the USA during 1996.

Three new-style dealerships have spearheaded 'System 2000' which links the showroom to Volvo UK at Marlow, Buckinghamshire, and to the factory in Gothenburg, Sweden. Within two years all Volvo dealers in America and Britain are intended to offer the revolutionary system.

Britain's *Daily Mail* described the experience in store for the first system users [49]:

> Volvo buyers will see pictured on an assembly screen their choice of car in 'undressed form' – without engine, transmission, wheels, interior trim, radio or personal features like colour and seat fabric. Buyers will build up their own car electronically to meet their personal requirements and price. And then, at the push of a button, the design will go to the Gothenburg [Sweden] car-build computer which will flash back a delivery date.

Volvo's objective with this interactive video system is to deliver a car in Europe within two weeks from the time of ordering. That would represent customer-pleasing progress.

'SYSTEM 2000'
PART OF PROFITABLE CHANGES AT VOLVO

Changing to a customer-responsive production system is just one of the many system improvements that have brought big benefits to the profitability of Volvo, especially in the USA. 'Changing the company in the way that it's been done is a big task – and it's been done much quicker than I thought possible,' says Mats Ola Palm, Chairman and CEO of Volvo Cars of North America Inc. [50].

'We've changed the company from a "push" system to a company that runs based on customer needs and demands – after 75 years of doing it the other way.' Palm adds, 'It used to be that at the end of the pipeline here [in retail] you had to sell what you produced. Now, we produce what we sell. That sounds like a fine point, but that's a helluva big difference.'

Mr Palm's remarks illustrate vividly the point of this chapter: by visualizing the customer standing at the end of the assembly line, building what they want when they want it, car makers satisfy not only their customers but also their shareholders.

POINTS FOR DISCUSSION AND REVIEW

- List six ways to reorganize production operations in human terms to help reduce costs.
- How can reduced design complexity contribute to a car company's ability to offer more models?
- Is the idea of building cars to specific customer order new in the auto industry?
- Are there ways to compensate the members of a production team according to the value of their contributions? Discuss.
- What planning and logistical tools can help reduce stocks of cars between the maker and the customer?
- Which car makers are pilot-testing car-ordering systems that put the customer in direct contact with the factory?

6 Customer-driven car selling

What exactly are the customer's wishes in automotive retailing? We need to know much more about their preferences for selecting and buying their personal transportation. Would they choose to reinvent the current system if it were to be started again from scratch? If so, how would they like to buy their cars?

Are car buyers happy trotting from one dealership to the next to see and price their future wheels? Or would customers be more satisfied by visiting one location to see a selection of various car ranges under one roof or in one complex? We consider these and other questions in this chapter.

SHOULD WE REINVENT THE CAR SELLING SYSTEM?

Fewer than one in five car buyers visits more than two car showrooms when seeking to buy a new car. In Britain in 1992 new and used car buyers visited an average of only 2.4 dealers before deciding where to buy their car. Does this mean that most have made their purchase decisions before entering the dealership?

In another survey, conducted in the UK by Pragma Strategic Marketing Consultants, 40% of buyers were found to have visited only one dealership to select the car they bought. This confirms that they find visiting dealerships to be much less convenient and enjoyable than car makers like to believe. Pragma also found that 39% of buyers had made up their mind about the marque and model they wanted before visiting a dealer; a further 35% made the decision at the dealership.

The implications of these findings for the achievement of customer satisfaction pose a number of questions. We have some answers from Europe and also from America, where experimentation with retail networks has been more active.

DEALER/MANUFACTURER
RELATIONSHIPS ARE DIFFICULT

Particularly when they are in a feisty frame of mind, car dealers are fond of saying that they are the real customers of the car makers and the final purchasers are their customers. Indeed, this role will be acknowledged by many car producers, who are often happier talking to dealers than to their final retail purchasers.

This characterization of the maker/dealer relationship is incomplete, however. The retail customer is free to go to a wide variety of dealers and to choose from all available car makes and models. The same freedom is not accorded to dealers. They are bound by a contractual relationship with their supplier or suppliers.

This relationship gives them certain rights and privileges but denies them the full freedom and indeed the potential purchasing power of retail customers, who can bargain between various outlets when they are selecting the best deal for their purchase. This is a real customer relationship – unlike the situation of car dealers, who are anything but free to bargain with their suppliers over the purchase of the products that they resell.

The implication here is that car makers must be more respectful of the position they occupy with respect to their dealers. Their contracts with dealers impose strict obligations on the latter. In compensation for this, they must be true to their side of the bargain. Indeed, they must strive to be more than true to their dealers, who can only be described as 'captive customers'.

DEALERS IN JAPANESE VOLUME MARQUES CAN
NEGLECT CUSTOMER SATISFACTION

When the cars are too good, dealers can get lazy. This is one of the clear lessons from the findings of a periodic J.D. Power study of the satisfaction of US customers with the sales experience. In 1987 when Power began researching sales satisfaction, dealers for Japanese imports were 31 index points worse than those for domestic models. Six years later the gap was still huge, although closer, at 26 index points.

In reporting on the findings, J. Ferron of Power said that the dealers in Japanese imports, long restricted in car supplies, had simply sat back and acted as 'order-takers'. Said Ferron [51], 'It's a showroom issue, coupled with higher prices. Customers demand more effective product knowledge and transfer of information.'

'As prices go up and domestic product quality improves,' Ferron added, 'something has to happen differently in [Japanese import] showrooms than is occurring now. There is a fully-engaged battle for satisfying people at the beginning of the relationship, starting at the showroom.'

HOW NOT TO HANDLE A CUSTOMER

An excellent example of the 'order-taker' mentality, blended in a lethal cocktail with all-too-familiar misogyny, was reported in Britain's *Daily Telegraph* by prospective woman buyer Fiona Hill [52]:

> The first salesman I spoke to seemed to have difficulty understanding when I said: 'I am interested in buying a Land Rover Discovery. Can you tell me about them?' I couldn't claim that he was rude, but he was completely uninterested in talking to me. If he'd bothered to ask I would have told him that I wanted the Discovery to replace my five-year-old Fiat Panda so that I could pull a horsebox and get to shows whatever the state of the fields.
>
> Perhaps my mistake was in admitting my ignorance of the world where macho-machines were bought and sold. More likely, I believe, he couldn't imagine a woman being seriously keen on buying this type of car. So I spoon-fed him. I asked if he had any second-hand vehicles and whether any were expected. I offered to visit his showroom, but he said that he didn't have anything to look at. I was told that I would be telephoned should anything suitable come in. That was four months ago. I haven't heard from him since.

Such 'selling' methods may be understandable (though only in the trade) when Discoverys are in short supply. But they will do little to prepare dealers and salespeople for the challenge of a buyers' market.

ZERO-DEFECT SELLING NEEDED
FOR ZERO-DEFECT CARS

When representatives of the German magazine *auto motor + sport* sought to gain some personal experience of the art and science of car buying they were dismayed by what they found. When their 'Mr Zendher' visited an Audi dealer in Neckarsulm, he found that only ten days before the official sales launch of the new top-range Audi A8 the Audi dealer there had no sales information available about the car. This, said the magazine's Ralph Alex, was 'The sorry result: no A8s will be sold, not even in Neckarsulm, where the A8 is in fact produced.'

The experiences of women, the magazine found, were particularly depressing. During one dealer visit, said a prospective woman buyer, 'After my request that someone show me the size of a car's trunk twenty minutes passed with no result.' Then she was asked by a salesman whether she belonged to the man who was standing nearby. 'No, I'm alone here,' she replied.

Speechless, the woman watched the salesman turn around and deal with the male customer instead of her. Heading for the exit door she shouted to the salesman, 'Nowhere in your advertising does it say that women are only served if they come with their husband or their parents!'

'These symptoms are diagnosed more and more often,' wrote Ralph Alex. 'One auto company to its horror discovered that only 14% of customers changed their dealers because they were unhappy with their cars. But 60% left a dealer because the sales staff took little interest in them. What use then is the zero-defect car built by the men in blue on the assembly line, if the white collars in sales produce trash?'

DEALER UPGRADING IN EUROPE AIDED BY NEW LUXURY RANGES

The same battle will be waged even more fiercely in European dealerships when Japanese-brand cars come into freer availability during the 1990s. Japanese importers face a long struggle to rid their dealerships of the 'order-taker' mentality of the restricted-import years and to help them gear up to the provision of real customer service.

Recognizing this, some Japanese marketers in Europe have used their new luxury-car ranges as 'carrots' to spur dealers to upgrade their facilities and personnel. Toyota's Lexus and Mazda's Xedos are both sold through main-marque dealerships. But dealers are not allowed to take on these ranges until they have met rigorous new standards

Fig. 6.1 Mazda used the European launch of its upmarket Xedos range (Xedos 6 SE shown) as the 'carrot' to persuade its dealers to upgrade their facilities and retrain their personnel.

for training, service, facilities and customer care. The upgrading in turn is intended to benefit the quality of selling of the volume Toyotas and Mazdas.

PEOPLE WILLING TO TRAVEL TO HAVE PLEASANT BUYING EXPERIENCE

What do we know about the preferences of consumers in car buying and servicing? The findings of a survey conducted by *Automotive News* in the USA disclosed that customers want their dealership to be less pressured, more understanding and more honest.

In terms of the facilities offered by a dealership they considered that having histories for their used cars was very important. Second in importance was a well-stocked parts department and third was the availability of trained and knowledgeable salespeople. As is so often the case, these findings underscore the importance of the service aspect of any dealership.

Research carried out to establish the Saturn network indicated that Americans were willing to travel 50 to 100 miles to buy a car, acknowledging the importance of such a major purchase to most families [53]. In the UK the Lex Report on Motoring found that 25% of new-car buyers were prepared to travel over 50 miles to buy a new car and 44% would drive over 20 miles.

This finding supports the idea that a car-buying trip could be a pleasure for the family as an outing for the day – if in fact it *is* a pleasure for them, not an experience that they dread. On the other hand it conflicts with the view that, in the USA at least, people don't have the time that they once had to dedicate to car buying.

Once upon a time the purchase of a car was one of the major family events. People would spend three or four hours in the dealership going through the details of the purchase and making the final arrangements for their new car. Many still enjoy this. In Japan, the trend is moving away from salespeople visiting customers' homes and towards customers visiting dealers to select new cars. This is especially true of the new generation of younger buyers.

COMING: MANY DIFFERENT WAYS TO BUY CARS

How are these conflicting concepts to be reconciled with the differing needs and desires of the consumer? Our conclusion is that in the buyers' market cars will be bought in many different ways to suit the needs of different kinds of consumers.

If they want to order their car through a buying service, from a catalogue without seeing or driving it, the customer will be able to do so. If they want to see and test-drive a variety of cars at a major dealer, they will be able to do that too.

If they want to sit at their PC and scroll through a choice of cars, prices and purchase options, they can do so. In the future there will be immense variety in the ways in which cars are sold, leased or rented to the consumer.

CALIFORNIA LEADING
IN USE OF BROKERAGE SERVICES

One straw in the wind is the growth of brokerage services in the USA. A broker works from your specification and gives you a price figure which you can then challenge a dealer to match. Alternatively the broker will acquire and deliver the car for you.

America's bellwether market, California, is showing a strong customer affinity for the pricing and purchases of cars through independent services. In California such services are licensed as used-car dealers.

A 1993 study by J.D. Power investigated the use by consumers of both pricing and buying services in California. Power found that against a national average of 4.5% of new-car buyers who bought their vehicle through a buying service, in California 10.0% made use of such services.

BUYER'S LOYALTY IS TO THE SERVICE USED

The main reason people used a buying service was to get what they thought was a lower price. They believed that they saved an average of $1800 by making use of a buying service. Other motivations were concerns over financing and a desire to avoid the hassle of a show-room visit.

The Power researchers concluded that the use of such services is generating a loyalty to the service, not to the dealer or the car maker. Of those buying through a referral organization, 93% said that they considered it an improvement over the usual way to buy a car. None said they thought it was worse.

The J.D. Power researchers concluded [54], 'Consumers want information from someone who's there to champion them. We need to ask how we can structure the franchise system differently so that customers feel they have someone helping them make these critical decisions.'

SHOPPING BY CABLE
REDUCES STORE AND INVENTORY COSTS

Another harbinger of this diversity is the booming popularity of 'home shopping' by cable television in the USA. *Business Week*'s Laura Zinn reports [55], 'It's already a $2-billion-plus industry and growing fast – about 20% a year. The ultimate vision: a sort of video mall, where shoppers will browse through TV channels as through individual stores, ask for information and advice, order, and pay – all without leaving the comforts of home.'

'Let me tell you the wonderful characteristics of home shopping,' Peter Siris, a UBS Securities analyst said to Laura Zinn. 'It's a low-cost distribution system. You don't need thousands of stores and you don't need thousands of pieces of inventory in each location.'

Home shopping for cars by cable TV may be less remote as a concept than it may at first appear. Auto makers seem convinced that television advertising well portrays the attributes of their products. Many promotional videos are already produced for sales promotion and training.

These video materials have only to be linked with the on-screen car-ordering networks being pilot-tested by Volvo, Rover, Ford and others (Chapter 5) to create an integrated selling, pricing and buying system. If the means are there, and if customers like it, the chances of implementation must be rated high.

EARLY TESTS OF CAR SHOPPING BY CABLE TV ARE INCONCLUSIVE

The sheer convenience of such a shopping method must draw the attention of the auto industry. An important factor in this respect could be the 12 to 16 weeks that customers typically spend considering the type of car they would like to buy before they first visit a dealership. To what extent could TV shopping techniques help a particular manufacturer establish a clear priority with the buyer during this critical period of secret contemplation?

One company willing to test the concept is General Motors. In late 1993 it joined forces to develop such a programme with Hachette Filipacchi Magazines, which publishes *Car and Driver* and *Road & Track*. Two hour-long programmes called *TV Car Showroom* ran on Cable Television's Home Shopping Network late in 1993.

GM, through its Pontiac Division, was the exclusive sponsor of the pilot shows. Cars were not to be sold directly by the programme, since GM is prevented by state laws and its relationships with dealers from selling cars directly to the public, bypassing its US dealer network. Instead the pilot programmes offered for $10 a certificate worth $500 of vehicle servicing. The certificate was valid for the servicing of a Pontiac car bought during a specified time period.

Thus the programme contents were intended to serve as a means of gathering a customer database – $10 was not too much to spend – as well as encouraging a potential car buyer to give more consideration to acquiring a Pontiac. In addition to items of clothing and licensed merchandise such a show was obviously adaptable to the sale of automotive accessories and various aftermarket products.

The pilot shows were intended to lead to the creation of a 24-hour automotive shopping channel to go on air in April 1994 through a selected cable system operator. However, *TV Car Showroom* did not have the desired impact. Thus this particular venture into TV shopping for cars did not make further progress.

LARGE MULTI-MARQUE 'CAR BARN' CONCEPT FOUND VALID

The Saturn research finding that customers are willing to travel some distance to have a pleasant car-buying experience gives some support to the concept of a large 'car barn' for selling, probably (though not necessarily) separated from service facilities. Thus in a particular area there could be one or two major centres for car selling and four, five or more centres strategically-located for service purposes. The latter would be factory-franchised outlets equipped and qualified to do warranty and service work.

The J.D. Power organization feels that beyond 2000 the network pattern will move toward dealers who each have a number of selling points and who sell a number of brands [56]. This suggests a move toward supermarket-style 'car barn' retailing that will make the brand-establishment challenge even greater for the car manufacturer. Importantly, the case can be made that a move in this direction will be liked by consumers because it will help them to shop more easily among various brands and models.

PRESENTATION POSSIBLE BY SEGMENT INSTEAD OF MARQUE

How should 'car barns' be organized? A customer-friendly approach would emulate that taken by supermarkets and department stores. Similar products would be displayed in separate areas: sports-car departments, 4×4 boutiques, luxury-car sections, diesel-car areas and so on. In fact in Sweden a plan is under way to set up a sport-utility 4×4 multi-brand dealership.

Such initiatives result in the opposite of the situation that is normally encountered by the consumer in a multi-brand dealership. Both car makers and, responding to their strictures, their contracted dealers will have tried to make it as difficult as possible for the customer to make clear comparisons between their vehicles and those offered by other makers.

However, car makers must believe that their product, brand reputation and service will stand up well against direct competition and comparison. Hence, the customer-friendly segment-focused presentation should be the environment they would most relish. If they do not relish it, they must urgently address their lack of competitiveness.

A specialized single-brand outlet has been put into practice in Japan by the Nissan Prince Tokyo Motor Sales Company. In June 1994 Nissan Prince set up a wholly-owned subsidiary selling only sport-utility vehicles, those produced by Nissan. They did so in part, they said, to meet the special information demands that such specialized customers have.

HOW TO OBTAIN BRAND DISTINCTION IN 'CAR BARNS'

Within 'car barns' the auto makers will seek to identify their areas and products distinctively. In the USA Volkswagen faces this problem. Once strongly exclusive, the VW brand is now almost 100% dualled with other marques. To give it clearer showroom identity VW implemented a promotion called 'Slice'.

In the 'Slice' system, a section of the showroom area is allocated to Volkswagen and completely redecorated at a cost of $25 000. VW pays outright for half of this and finances the rest for the dealer. VW will also finance the expenditure of $75 000 on the rest of the showroom over a 36-month period for the general improvement of the selling environment.

TRADITIONAL DEALERSHIPS BENEFIT FROM INTELLIGENT OVERHAUL

Car makers and their dealers are stepping up their attention to the aesthetics, layout and operation of the conventional singleton dealership. Pontiac General Sales and Service Manager Elwood Schlesinger explained why [57]: 'Customer satisfaction begins with the first impression – the look and feel of the facility. Customers want to shop in an environment that is clean, exciting and fun, just like when they visit a retail shopping mall.'

In 1989, Pontiac created and promoted a new plan and look for its dealerships. Since then, 200 have been remodelled along the new lines. The benefits have been strikingly consistent: every single one of these 200 outlets has reported increases in sales and profits as well as improvements in customer satisfaction. Higher employee morale and productivity have also followed.

SATURN AND LEXUS ARE SETTING NEW DEALER DESIGN STANDARDS

Another GM division, Oldsmobile, is planning to follow some of the dealer planning leads established successfully by Saturn. At a Saturn outlet, the reception area is given the welcoming feel of a hotel lobby. Business customers can make use of work stations and a toy box is a

Fig. 6.2 Toyota's dedicated Lexus showrooms in the USA emphasize clean, open spaces and glass instead of poster-bedecked walls so that the product is the centre of the buyer's focus.

welcome distraction for young children. Instead of being crammed in a showroom, where only a few models are shown, the Saturn range is displayed on a plaza in front of the dealership.

Toyota's Lexus has designed its dealerships to enhance customer satisfaction, reported Michelle Krebs [57]: 'The customer is greeted by a receptionist. A salesperson is called from an office into the showroom. The showroom, with its vaulted ceiling, has glass-panelled closing offices in the corners. The idea of glass instead of walls is to keep the customer's eyes fixed on the product.'

In the design of car dealerships we are entering an era in which more fantasy than ever before is not only feasible but desirable. In France, for example, the design studio of Iosa Ghini was engaged to plan new types of dealership interiors in a postmodern style.

Dramatic design elements of anodized aluminium and unusual forms characterized the proposal by Iosa Ghini, which will have an extremely strong appeal to younger customers. By the same token it would also be an environment in which younger and smarter sales and service personnel would enjoy working – no minor consideration.

MATCHING SALESPEOPLE TO CUSTOMERS IMPROVES RELATIONSHIPS

When the salesperson emerges from the office, he or she should complement the brand they represent. It is disadvantageous for the

American domestic marques that their salespeople are 'appreciably older' than those selling imported cars [53]. These salespeople have no personal comprehension of what the new generation of buyers wants and why it wants it.

In contrast, some salespeople for the import brands (and now Saturn as well) are dedicated 'zealots'. They believe earnestly and sincerely that people should want and need the cars that they are selling.

Mr Duncan Brodie, GM's Director of Dealer Systems and Communications, is aware of the problem [58]: 'Dealers have an enormous problem with sales personnel turnover. At the same time, the products are becoming more complex, and there is a tremendous demand on salespeople to know all the answers. That is further compounded by multiple franchises – a salesperson has to know not only all of our information but everybody else's too.'

The problem of needing to know all the answers is being addressed by the Nissan Sunny Tokyo Auto Sales Company, which has 60 outlets in the Tokyo area. It is giving intensive product training to a cadre of experts in its various outlets. These experts are being trained to be able to answer any and all questions and particularly to offer rebuttals to negative claims made by the competition.

COMPUTERIZED SALES SUPPORT SYSTEMS BEING TESTED

General Motors is beginning to pilot-test a computerized selling system that could help fill the information gap. It calls it Sales-Assist-Manager. The system uses laser disc technology and is being developed by two of GM's divisions, Hughes Electronics Corporation and Electronic Data Systems Corporation (EDS).

Installed in a dealership, the Sales-Assist-Manager system can be updated daily by GM's direct Pulsat satellite link to 8735 of its dealerships. About 7500 of its dealerships are also able to receive video programmes by satellite.

'The day of the hotshot salesman wheeling and dealing to make a sale has to end,' said GM's Brodie. 'Our belief is that if customers are able to call up all the information they need on a screen and see it for themselves, they are more likely to trust the information. It is going to change the way we do business, because it takes the pressure off the salesperson.'

COMPUTER CAN GO TO THE CUSTOMER

An alternative brings the television screen and a company representative to the customer. A system serving this purpose was developed for a truck producer by CWC Inc. in Mankato, Minnesota. The truck company's sales representative brings a laptop computer to the client.

Sitting together, using a graphics-based program developed by CWC, they can 'build' a truck on the screen by making choices from a menu of hardware choices and colour schemes. The program is capable of showing the appearance of the resulting truck, computing its price and analysing various financing options. The resulting information can then be transmitted to a central location for action.

NO SUBSTITUTE FOR INTENSIVE TRAINING

Computerized information retrieval may well assist salespeople. But with American research indicating that the various customer-handling skills of the individual salesperson account for 70% of the factors that satisfy the customer at the time of purchase, effective training of sales-people must take a high priority.

Infiniti, the Japanese franchise most liked in this respect by the American car buyer, attributes its success to the training programmes it conducts for its dealership employees. It has recently intensified its effort to be sure that its salespeople are well informed about its products and those of its rivals.

'Since its beginning in 1989,' reported Mark Rechtin in *Automotive News* [51], 'Infiniti has taken all dealership employees to a six-day training course in Scottsdale, Arizona to teach product knowledge and people skills. Infiniti customer service representatives also call every person who buys a car to ensure he or she is satisfied with the purchase.'

SALES TRAINING CHRYSLER-STYLE

Contractor Ross Roy operates Chrysler's new 'Customer One' pro-gramme for improving customer satisfaction through better dealer performance. Launched on 29 June 1992, Customer One received a $30 million Chrysler input in that and subsequent years. The cost to the dealer is $100 for each trainee.

The launch of Customer One paralleled the introduction of Chrys-ler's new LH-series cars. 'Chrysler figured that its new cars would attract customers who had never considered a Chrysler product and others who would return to Chrysler to give the company another chance,' reports Arlena Sawyers [59]. 'The company knew it couldn't afford to disappoint customers again. That meant customer service had to improve.'

Training sessions take place over one or two days, depending on the person's job in the dealership. 'The training focuses on self-discovery via role playing and team exercises,' writes Sawyers. 'Participants learn to put themselves in the shoes of the customer and the importance of being up-front and truthful.' The training sessions are followed by further Customer One actions in the dealerships, where employees hone their customer-pleasing strengths.

Participation has been high: by the end of February 1994 110 000 people at 3800 Chrysler dealerships had been trained in the Customer One programme. Said a Chrysler manager, 'People who in the past might not have been trained are now in the forefront of creating a relationship between the dealership and the customer.'

WITH INCENTIVES, CUSTOMER ONE IS WORKING

Thomas Marinelli, Chrysler Director of Sales and Marketing Training, administers the company's 'Drive for the Gold' programme linked with Customer One. He can pay out some $200 million a year in incentives to dealers, depending on the customer satisfaction ratings they achieve. However, Marinelli emphasizes that the real benefit to dealers who improve their customer satisfaction scores will be repeat purchasers and referrals from happy owners – a theme we sanction and develop further in the next chapter.

Chrysler's methods were endorsed by Warner Moore, a customer relations manager with a Dodge dealership. Joseph Bohn reports [60]:

> He said he was sceptical about anyone teaching him to handle problems which, as a sales manager, he had run across every day. But Moore was surprised. 'One thing that really stuck: you find the problem and resolve it at any cost. When I first heard that, I thought, "You're out of your mind." But that's what we've done. When a problem arises, we determine whose fault it was and that department is held accountable.'

Chrysler's Executive Vice President of Sales and Marketing, Theodore Cunningham, said that his studies have shown correlation of the training with improved internal CSI scores. He also said that Chrysler was getting fewer letters of complaint and more expressing compliments. 'That says this is working and the customers are noticing,' stated Cunningham [59]. 'We haven't changed all the minds in the company or in the dealership organisation, but we are making sound progress.'

With the launch of its new small car, the Neon, Chrysler moved into a new phase of Customer One. Neon training was conducted in dealerships, bringing in competitive cars such as Saturn, Ford Escort and Honda Civic for direct comparisons with the Neon.

MORE PROFESSIONALISM
TO FIGHT HIGH SALES-STAFF TURNOVER

Since expenditures for training are rising and must rise, a major concern is the high turnover of dealer sales staff. In America sales staff turnover exceeds 50% a year [61]. Yet this is happening at a time when customers have more time and are being provided with much more information to develop their own ideas about the information they need to make a car-buying decision. Only an intelligent conversation with a knowledgeable salesperson will satisfy the demanding 'professional customer'.

To fight high sales-staff turnover, the US car dealer association (NADA) has launched a sales-staff certification programme. Its objective is to train and certify dealer sales staff to give their job more real and implied professionalism. Better professionalism on the part of salespeople helps substantially to improve their rates of success, the dealers believe.

Another approach to the retention of sales staff and their loyalty is adopted by Volkswagen: it pays salespeople $150 per car sold and spreads the payment over a three-year period. If the salesperson leaves the Volkswagen franchise they forfeit the balance of any payments owed them.

NEW FORMS OF INCENTIVES ARE NEEDED

A method of incentivizing salespeople to work with and help retain existing customers has been put into use by a US dealer. If one of their salespeople sells to a customer who bought his previous car from the dealership, even as long as five years ago, they receive an extra 10% commission. The amount paid would be small, the dealer believes, in relation to the amount they would need to spend on advertising to attract new customers if they did not enjoy strong repeat business.

The system of paying car salespeople a commission tends to work strongly in favour of the needs of the salesperson as a priority over the customer's needs. One proposal to adjust the balance is that salespeople should be paid a fixed rate of commission on all their vehicle sales. If they are paid a fixed amount, whether or not they are selling a new or used car or whether the profit is large or small, they will be selling the car that is best for the customer and for the dealer.

The introduction of such a system could mesh well with the changes in pricing policies of both car producers and their dealers. In addition it could work more effectively with a less vertically-organized dealership, one in which anyone on the staff could have an opportunity to sell a car or a service.

Crucially important in the development of sound customer-satisfying techniques is that any financial rewards offered for good performance are fully compatible with the values that are taught in parallel. 'Despite all this training,' says one analyst of dealer systems, 'most dealers haven't changed their pay plans and the employees will do what they're paid to do. The manufacturers are sending two messages and the dealer will always pick the one that makes the most money – incentives are usually stronger than training.'

STRICT STAFF STANDARDS
CAN AND SHOULD BE ENFORCED

Coddling sales staff is not the answer, suggests the experience of Longo Toyota, America's largest car dealer. When they join Longo, sales staff sign a code of ethics which is rigorously enforced. 'If they lie to a customer, we fire them,' says Longo president Greg Penske [62]. 'Our staff are not allowed to smoke or wear sunglasses at work and they have to adhere to a dress code. All these things give the right impression.'

That the impression is the right one is indicated by Longo's amazing repeat business ratio. Penske: 'About 80% of our business at Longo is referral and repeat business. I'd say the average dealership is getting 10% to 20%.' Does this help lower the marketing costs of this huge ($500 million annual turnover) Los Angeles dealership? You bet it does.

Another successful dealership, Sewell Village Cadillac in Texas, practises balance in its relationships with its employees. 'Treating employees with respect doesn't mean you have to be weak,' writes dealer principal Carl Sewell [63]. 'You can be firm without being rude. We don't have to swear at people to get them to do something. We ask politely. If that doesn't get them to do the job, we'll get someone else who will. After that happens a couple of times, everybody gets the message.'

HOW HARD WORK AT THE RITZ-CARLTON
MAKES CUSTOMER CARE LOOK EASY

An outstanding example of staff training and motivation leading to business success is provided by the 27-unit Ritz-Carlton hotel chain. Although the pay of the Ritz-Carlton's 11 500 employees differs little from that at other hotels, the company rewards exceptional performance with fully-paid vacations and other perks. As a result its employee turnover averages 30%, lower than the 45% of other luxury hotel chains.

What's the secret? Training, training and more training, combined with high standards and motivation. 'The two-day orientation [for new employees], which is held each week, is just the beginning,' wrote Edwin McDowell [64]. 'Employee indoctrination at Ritz-Carlton Hotel Company includes 100 additional hours of training, daily inspections for appearance, performance reviews and an unrelenting emphasis on quality.'

'The Ritz-Carlton is in a class by itself,' said M.L. Smith, professor at the University of Nevada's College of Hotel Administration. 'They have figured out what guests want in a hotel, and they have learned how to exceed their expectations.' This helped the Ritz-Carlton hold its occupancy rate at 70.2% in 1992, when average occupancy in the

USA dropped to 61.7% from 62.6% in 1989. Ritz-Carlton was one of the organizations that Chrysler studied to develop its Customer One programme.

SALESPEOPLE OPERATE AS TEAMS IN JAPAN TO ASSIST CUSTOMERS

In Japan, some 20% of car dealerships are directly factory-owned and more are partially owned by the car makers. This represents a much higher direct ownership by the car makers of retail dealer operations than is the case in any other major market.

The Japanese selling system is highly labour-intensive. In the Japanese system the salesperson is not so much of a 'lone wolf' as their counterpart in the West. They are more a member of a selling team which shares all the commissions earned. Like someone selling insurance, Japanese car salespersons seek to position themselves as an advocate of the customer's needs rather than as a representative of the car maker.

Japanese salespeople know far more about their present and potential customers than their counterparts in the rest of the world. They have their own databases on clients and their families. In addition, in Japan many car owners carry a 'smart card' which provides their details – their employment, family, car-ownership history and so on.

REAL TEAMWORK NEEDS SUPPORTING TRAINING

Improving co-operation and teamwork is the aim of the exercises in which Saturn and Oldsmobile dealers participate in a special training camp 25 miles northwest of Orlando, Florida. Run by Saturn, the 'Excel' training activity includes three days of lectures and outside exercises in physical co-operation among the participants.

The objective is to develop trust, the kind of trust that is needed, for example, if a group of dealers in a metropolitan area are to adopt a fixed-price selling system. They must have confidence that one dealer won't break from the agreed concept. They must develop mutual trust at the management level as well as trust to aid teamwork within their organizations.

The specialized Excel teamwork training, resembling an Outward Bound exercise, has the potential to build trust and co-operation within the staff of an individual dealership. If true teamwork is to be achieved it will need to be reinforced and developed by specialized training activities above and beyond strict professional responsibilities.

JAPANESE LOOKING TO REDUCE SELLING COSTS

The structure of car selling is changing in Japan for several reasons. Younger buyers are more interested in visiting special lifestyle showrooms to consider new cars and less attuned to the traditional house-calls by salespeople.

When the car was delivered it would be done personally and the purchaser would hand over a wad of yen. But, said a spokesman for Toyota [65], 'customs are becoming more "dry" now. People are paying by bank transfers. Little by little, they are not so interested in personal delivery directly from the salesperson.'

In recognition of this change, reported Mary Anne Maskery, 'Toyota's Toyopet channel is trying a new delivery system that it hopes will save $11.8 million a year. From now on, the salesperson will not drive a new car to a customer's home so he can personally turn over the keys. Instead, a driver from the pre-delivery inspection yard will deliver the car. Toyopet is hoping the system will eliminate parking fees required when vehicles are stored at dealers located in Japan's crowded cities. They're also hoping to cut down on sales-staff work hours.'

MAJORITY OF NEW-CAR CUSTOMERS DISLIKE PRICE HAGGLING

Auto selling is the only important retailing sector in Europe where prices are still the subject of haggling. Yet many customers neither ask for, nor necessarily expect, a discount. Whether a discount is available will depend on the conditions of supply and demand in the marketplace coupled with the incentives in play for the dealership and salesperson at the moment of sale.

Research into buyer opinions in the British market conducted by Mori on behalf of the Lex Group, a major car distribution company, shows that three out of five new-car buyers would prefer being offered a lower fixed list price than a higher one from which they were to negotiate an individual discount.

The survey covered nearly 1300 UK drivers, of whom only a minority was comfortable haggling for a discount. The split for male and female drivers showed that only 28% of women actually enjoyed negotiating, against half the men.

According to J.D. Power, a 32% overall share of car buyers in the USA like to negotiate. The remaining two thirds, say the researchers [66], 'dislike the negotiation process and distrust automotive sales-people'. The Power group considers that 'consumer dissatisfaction with the current system is so great that dealers and manufacturers will have to respond.'

HAGGLE-FREE FIXED PRICING
PIONEERED BY DEALERS

More associated with the hustle and hassle of street markets, negotiating over price is psychologically inconsistent with the factual, customer-friendly atmosphere that a modern auto showroom needs. Certainly it is against the interests of customers. When there is no transparency of selling prices they must suspect that they are not getting the best possible value for money.

An alternative method, fixed or 'no-haggle' pricing, has been pioneered by car dealers. It significantly reduces the amount of time that has to be spent negotiating the financial deal. This makes selling more efficient for the dealer and more enjoyable for the customer. The actual final deal, of course, also depends on the value given to a traded-in car. Thus scope for negotiation remains even in a fixed-price selling environment.

A pioneer of the 'no-haggle' approach has been Gordon Stewart, a Chevrolet dealer in Detroit and Chairman of Stewart Management Group. Such pricing, he told the *Automotive News* World Congress, is defined as the practice of:

● setting the lowest acceptable selling price;
● clearly posting the price on each vehicle;
● firmly adhering to that price when selling.

Stewart reported improved sales from the technique at his Garden City, Michigan dealership. With traditional methods he sold 1123 new cars in 1987. Adopting the no-dicker sticker at the end of the year, he increased sales to 2248 units in 1989. The dealership's CSI rating rose from 84% in 1987 to 91% in 1992. Based on their individual CSI ratings, Stewart's salespeople are awarded a bonus. They also receive volume bonuses in addition to their salary.

US DEALERS ADOPTING NO-HAGGLE PRICING

At the beginning of 1992 J.D. Power and the NADA estimated that some 10 dealerships in the USA had begun to use 'no-haggle' or fixed posted prices. In a later survey, however, Power reported that in fact 974 dealers had experimented with fixed pricing in 1991. The number increased to 1665 dealers in 1992, about 10% of US dealerships, and then declined slightly to a 9% share in 1993. This was taken as an indication that dealers were continuing to experiment with fixed-price selling but that it was not necessarily suitable for use by all dealers in all locations.

In the USA, 63% of dealers said that they considered that fixed-price selling had the ability to generate new vehicle sales, against only 5% who felt the contrary. More than half also felt that fixed-price selling contributed to the generation of profit on new vehicle sales.

PROS AND CONS OF FIXED PRICING

In a mid-1992 study J.D. Power interviewed a focus group of 24 dealers who were using fixed pricing. Of these, 65% said that they practise no-haggle on new cars only, while 35% said that prices are fixed for both new and used cars. Among their findings were the following:

- Of the dealers studied, 92% said that their sales had increased since they adopted no-dicker stickers.
- Half the dealers said that their average gross profits have increased since they started pricing firmly, a quarter said the new pricing had not affected gross profits and the remaining quarter reported that their grosses had fallen.
- Of the dealers studied, 54% said that they still reserve the right to negotiate the values of cars being traded in, this of course being a key variable in any no-haggle pricing scheme.

No-dicker stickers are not for everyone. In a dense urban area where many dealers of the same make are competing for business a fixed price could be virtually impossible to enforce. This is the view of Longo Toyota's Greg Penske [62]: 'There are 75 Toyota dealers in the Los Angeles region. We do almost 16% of the Toyota retail business between San Diego and Santa Barbara but in this area you could hit 14 Toyota stores in an hour. A fixed-price guy could not survive in that environment.'

FIXED-PRICE SELLING HELPS SELL
PRODUCT AND SERVICE, NOT JUST THE DEAL

Responding to the findings of its own survey, mentioned above, Britain's Lex Group began testing fixed-price selling in 1993. 'Even more people than were indicated in our survey will prefer not to haggle once they have tried it,' said Sir Trevor Chinn, Lex Service Chairman and Chief Executive [67]. 'Fixed pricing means you end up selling a product and level of service to customers and not just a price.'

Said a US dealer, 'Fixed-price selling represents the transformation from a culture of conquest to a culture of conscience. It attempts to remove the adversarial relationship with the customer.' Dealer Gordon Stewart says that customers like no-dicker pricing because they feel comfortable knowing that everyone who is buying the same model and options is paying the same price.

'There is a group of dealers who now say, "this is what consumers want," ' said another US dealer [68]. 'They have increased awareness so that even dealers who don't have a no-negotiation policy are modifying their approach with consumers.'

CONGENIAL ATMOSPHERE
FOR BOTH BUYER AND SELLER

This changed selling atmosphere is more congenial for both buyers and sellers. Large dealers in Colorado and Texas reported to Jean-Charles Robin of the Phoenix Group that since adopting fixed pricing they have been receiving applications from salespeople with distinctly higher intellectual and educational qualifications [69]. They too are attracted by the emphasis on selling product and service instead of price that the no-haggle system promotes.

The only motor company that is firmly committed throughout its operations to fixed pricing is Saturn in the USA. Saturn salespeople find that this greatly facilitates their ability to get to know a potential Saturn purchaser.

Said one Saturn salesman, 'They're not arguing with me. I'm a stranger to them. They don't have to sit down here and argue with me about a car. It makes it a lot easier for both of us. If you've got a lot of tension, they're worried you're going to rip them off. Normally customers hate buying a car.'

This is a key consideration in favour of fixed pricing: it makes the procedure more agreeable for the salesperson as well as the customer. If the aim of the industry is to attract and keep quality sales staff, as it must be, the professionalism of the job must be enhanced. Only by eliminating the 'trading bazaar' approach to car selling will it be possible to hire and train professional people who are able to take pride in their work. And only with pride will come long-term commitment to the job.

NO-HAGGLE PRICING REQUIRES NERVES OF STEEL

In the UK market, where the fixed-price method had yet to be fully evaluated, reservations were expressed by Alan Pulham, Head of the Retail Motor Industry's Franchised Retailer Division [67]: 'A large operator retailing 1000 cars a year could make the scheme work, but our organisation is made up of dealers and they will always deal. Fixed pricing appeals to powerful dealer groups and manufacturers for different reasons, but the grass-roots retail industry will resist it.'

One reason for such resistance is the difficulty of making the change. Comprehensively converting to fixed-price selling is not easy, dealers report. 'Converting to fixed-price is the most severe gut-wrenching process anyone in the industry can go through,' said one US dealer. 'Once you get into it, you look at every aspect of your business and ask, "Is this consistent with my business philosophy?"'

But the change must be made, continued the dealer: 'The boom times of the 1980s have levelled off. In this mature market, we can't harvest customers like wheat any more. We don't get three or four crops a year. We need to keep our customers and customer base.

We felt it was time to stop treating customers like passing prey. It is the right way to treat people and do business.'

Dealers heavily committed to fixed-price selling use the same technique to price all aspects of their dealership operations, including used vehicles, trade-ins, accessories, chemical products and service contracts. Doing so adds additional assurance to the concept encouraged by fixed-price selling that no one else is getting a better deal. All customers, whether rich or poor, are treated alike by the dealerships.

'ONE-PRICE SELLING' FOR MODEL RANGES PIONEERED IN EUROPE

Fixed or no-haggle pricing is often confused with another technique which is correctly given the name of 'one-price selling'. In a one-price-selling programme, pricing is simplified by posting a single retail price for which a buyer can obtain a variety of models or power units. One-price selling must be initiated by the auto makers, since it must apply to a national or at least a regional market where it can be effectively launched and promoted through the media. Ford has used this technique successfully in Europe with its Fiesta and Escort, particularly in France.

In the USA Ford is offering its Escort LX in various body styles at a single price and is considering expanding the programme to other models. It has adopted a modified one-price policy for its Thunderbird LX range. Mitsubishi in the USA has been trying to use 'one-price' concepts to make purchasing easier in its dealerships. It has tested a single-price lease system to make financing less confusing. Its dealers have been pushing Mitsubishi to adopt a one-price policy for its Mirage range.

Confusingly, dealers would be free to adopt their own no-haggle price level for the sale of a car priced under a car maker's one-price policy. Thus the clear distinction between the two types of pricing must be drawn.

PHENOMENAL SUCCESS FOR NEW REBATE-GENERATING CREDIT CARD

In the USA, General Motors caused a tremendous stir by launching a GM-branded MasterCard credit card. It began offering the GM MasterCard in September 1992 and in February 1993 added a GM Gold MasterCard. The credit-card industry was astounded by the speed with which people have taken up the GM-branded product. It is ranked as the fastest-ever card launch, having won 4.9 million card-holders by mid-1993.

Use of the card offers specific advantages to the holder. When a cardholder buys a new General Motors car, he or she is entitled to a rebate on the price equal to 5% of the amount spent to date on that card, up to a maximum of $3500 (£2200) over seven years. This rebate is granted in addition to any discount on the car that the customer may achieve in haggling with his dealer.

GM CARD IS ALREADY 'TURNING PLASTIC INTO STEEL'

GM's objective with the card is to improve both sales and customer loyalty. The card is promoted with the promise of 'turning plastic into steel'. First indications are that it is more than achieving its goals. From the launch of the GM Card in September 1992 through March 1994, 140 000 cars and trucks were sold to buyers using rebates earned with their card.

'The Card is selling cars,' says Ronald Zeebeck, Managing Director of GM's credit card operations [70]. 'We have pulled people into the market earlier than we would have anticipated. This is creating a predictable core base of people who are going to buy cars each year for the next seven years.' Turning plastic into steel? The alchemists of old would applaud the success of GM's customer-pleasing credit card.

GM has been delighted to discover that people using the card rebates are younger and financially better off than GM's average buyer. In addition, the card is appealing strongly in two regions where GM sales are relatively weak: New York and California.

GM reported that the card was more successful than expected in attracting buyers to GM from other brands: four to five times as many converts as it had forecast. In California, one of GM's weaker markets, fully half of the rebate-using purchasers were not driving GM cars.

USE OF CARD DATABASE FOR DIRECT MARKETING

With more than 10 million people using the GM card early in 1994, GM was beginning to use this massive database for other marketing programmes. 'Now we're moving into some bold and brave new areas of how to develop our database,' said Philip Guarascio, GM General Manager of Marketing and Advertising. 'It's going to be a laser-scalpel kind of marketing.'

A first step was the sharing of information from the database with dealers. Dealers were provided with printouts of GM Card holders in their territories. Also they received lists of those purchasers who made use of the rebate so the dealers could follow up with appropriate offers of warranty coverage and service provision.

Ford countered GM with a similar card offering lower rates of interest and a maximum rebate value attained after five years rather than seven. Ford admitted that its entry into the branded credit-card market was 'somewhat defensive'. It took the measure to prevent the

GM Card from eroding the loyalty of Ford owners. Since the Ford programme is run in partnership with Citibank, which maintains the database, its list of cardholders is less accessible to Ford for direct-marketing purposes.

CREDIT CARD CONCEPT VALID IN EUROPE TOO

In the wake of its tremendous marketing success in the USA with the GM Card, GM's Vauxhall subsidiary launched a GM Card in Britain in the Autumn of 1993. Although General Motors is less well known as a brand in Britain than Vauxhall, GM deliberately chose the 'GM' label for the card to communicate the concept that this is a general-use credit card, not a card that may only be used for vehicle-related purchases.

For every pound spent on the British GM Card, five pence accumulates in points to a ceiling of £500 per year. These may be accumulated over a maximum of five years, generating £2500 to use toward the purchase of a new car. Britain's high proportion of company-car

Fig. 6.3 Instead of the car brand 'Vauxhall' the more neutral name 'GM Card' was chosen in the UK to avoid any impression that the credit card was for auto-related purchases only.

drivers was also catered to. They can redeem their rebate points at such general retailers as Currys, Next and Dixons.

One month after the official launch of the card in January 1994, and after a £15 million marketing spend, the GM Card had more than 250 000 members in the UK. This was considered a very successful launch in a market that is already saturated with credit-card carriers. Now will plastic be turned into steel as quickly in Europe as it was in America? It would be unwise to bet against it.

POINTS FOR DISCUSSION AND REVIEW

- To whom does the customer 'belong' and why: the car maker or the dealer?
- How can the launches of new ranges of cars be used to upgrade dealer operations?
- Many different ways of selling cars will be used in the future: list and describe as many as you can.
- What is meant by 'matching salespeople to customers'?
- Summarize the evidence that intensive dealer training contributes to improved customer relations.
- Define the difference between 'fixed pricing' of cars and 'one-price' selling.

7 Customer-driven car servicing

After-sales service is by far the richest potential area for the improvement of customer relations and the development of customer-friendly relations on the part of car companies and their dealers. But the way forward to first-class service is not always clear. In this chapter we seek to chart a profitable course.

QUALITY CARS
CAN PRODUCE COMPLACENT DEALERS

It is perhaps no surprise that top-level service has been a way of life in Japan for decades. Accordingly, Japanese cars are designed and built to require as little non-routine service as possible. This has also strongly supported the global export drive from Japan. An American Honda dealer who also owns several domestic franchises says [21], 'When customers bring their Hondas in for the 7500-mile checkup, they say: "I don't know what you are supposed to do to my car, but please don't mess it up. It is running great just the way it is." '

As noted earlier, however, this has its downside: it allows dealers to relax. They no longer have to perform a rigorous pre-delivery inspection (PDI). They can assume that satisfied customers will return for another Japanese car. Ironically, product competence can and does breed a dangerous servicing complacency.

WHEN PRODUCTS HAVE PROBLEMS,
SERVICE MUST BE STRESSED

The converse holds true: when products have problems, service must step up to the challenge if the brand is not to suffer permanent damage. The worst situations arise when the products are causing quality problems in the field and dealers consider that the car company has left them 'holding the bag'.

'In the early 1980s,' Cadillac dealer Carl Sewell told *Automobile* [71], 'Cadillac's products missed their mark. If it had not been for the excellent service people at Cadillac, it would have been touch and go, but [Assistant General Sales Manager] Bill Lewellen provided the customer care that was desperately needed when the product wasn't so good.'

As part of its programme to meet the needs of customers with troubled Cadillacs, the GM division was the first US car marketer to provide roadside service 24 hours a day, seven days a week with customer access via a hotline. Cadillac's policies are discussed in more detail later in the chapter.

Along with Lexus, said dealer Sewell, Cadillac is one of 'the best service providers for the customer. Most things should be for the customer, because he or she will determine whether the dealer and the manufacturer stay in business.'

When many of its cars were suffering from service problems in the 1980s, our surveys showed that Britain's Rover was reluctant to give its dealers the service support that they needed to satisfy customers. This both demoralized the dealers and upset the customers. Rover learned its lesson. It has since reversed those policies to become one of Europe's most customerized car makers.

ENCOURAGING OWNERS TO COMPLAIN: THE KEY TO BETTER SERVICE

In the USA the state of Florida follows up on problems that car owners consider to be chronic. This monitoring is needed as part of Florida's 'lemon law' programme which triggers an arbitration process that could oblige car makers to repair or repurchase defective cars.

Florida officials report that Oldsmobile and Buick have very low rates of reports of chronic defects. This was attributed by the administrator of the programme to the fast response of these companies to owner complaints: 'Problems are quickly resolved.' Clearly these GM divisions are determined to support their dealers in carrying out fast rectification to keep owners happy.

In fact, every possible effort must be made to persuade customers to complain. Encouraging customer complaints has been found very effective in increasing the opportunity for repeat business – and customer problems are most often encountered at the service level.

According to research in the USA, only 40 of every 100 dissatisfied customers will be moved to complain about their problem. Of these, 20 will be satisfied by the dealer and will repurchase their brand. A further eight customers will repurchase even though they judge that they are still not fully satisfied. Of the 60 in 100 dissatisfied customers who don't complain, only six will repurchase the same make.

Clearly, the task of the dealer is to encourage customers to complain. Once a customer has complained the opportunity is presented to work with them and achieve satisfaction. If in the process the dealer can go beyond satisfaction to delight or enthusiasm, the potential for a longer-lasting relationship is created.

THE GOAL:
MIX FINE SERVICE WITH FIRST-CLASS PRODUCT

During the after-sales period Longo Toyota Lexus in El Monte, California bends over backward to take a positive approach to customer satisfaction. 'Nowadays you have to sell your facility instead of just selling on price,' Longo president Greg Penske told *Motor Trader* [62]. 'People are definitely prepared to pay a little more to buy through a dealer that will look after you if something goes wrong.'

Longo personnel speak to as many as 40 000 customers a year on the telephone to find out if they are satisfied with their cars and service. 'We are not waiting for them to call us,' said Penske. 'We are on the offensive – being pro-active. Our new-vehicle sales department at Longo scores 97.1% on CSI ratings. But I don't regard 97.1% as satisfactory. We've got to go for 100%.'

Combining fine products with first-class customer care has helped make Longo America's largest dealer, indeed with bragging rights to claim to be the largest single retail auto outlet in the world. In 1992 Longo's 25-acre site sold more than 17 000 new Toyotas, 4000 used Toyotas and 18 000 Lexuses – fleet sales excluded.

OUTSTANDING SERVICE
CAN LINK CUSTOMER TO DEALER

The importance of good service to vehicle sales is underlined again and again. According to a survey in Germany, two out of three satisfied service customers intend to buy their new or used car in the dealership where they are a service customer.

Robert Shook quotes Honda's senior vice-president of auto operations, Tom Elliott [21]: 'Our research shows that the price of a car is not the most important reason why people buy from a particular dealer – outstanding service is. The average customer will pay more to a dealer with whom he or she has experienced good service in the past.' According to Shook:

Honda believes that the three most important contacts a car owner has with a dealership are:

1. The sales person who sells the car.
2. The service advisor to whom the customer brings the car for servicing.
3. The cashier the customer pays when doing business with the dealership.

Britain's Retail Motor Industry Federation (RMIF) commissioned a major survey of customers to measure their satisfaction with auto dealers in the early 1990s. The RMIF reported a strong correlation between owners' satisfaction with their cars and the overall rating that they gave to their dealer's service department. This is further confirmation of the important role of service in overall customer satisfaction.

The respondents to the RMIF survey were not impressed by the 'soft' aspects of the service experience. Although the showroom facilities and the performance of the service reception personnel was considered important, they judged their evaluation of servicing chiefly on the performance of the service workshop. Getting the car fixed to their satisfaction was their main priority.

NEW FORD AND GENERAL MOTORS CUSTOMER-SERVICE PRIORITIES

How closely General Motors sees servicing as being linked with selling was explained by John N. Costin, Executive Director of its European Parts and Accessories operation [72]:

> Success in the new-car market is becoming more and more dependent upon how well the customer is treated during the ownership period. There are no bad cars any more. The car buyer expects nothing less than a superior product. Winners in our industry will be those that provide something extra, something 'more than expected.'
>
> The customer experience during car ownership – the 'softer' side of our business – is becoming more and more important and it is this area that will make the difference in the future. It's an area that embraces all aspects of owning a car – from the time the customer decides to purchase a car to the time he changes the car and buys another one.
>
> We regard all the phases involved in selecting, purchasing, owning, selling, and repurchasing a car as an integral part of a continuous decision-making process. In fact, we regard after-sales as very much a key selling tool within the whole process.

'We have identified some highly critical areas that we believe are the most important drivers when it comes to being a leader in customer satisfaction,' Costin added. 'Some of these areas are pretty fundamental to our business and include offering the best levels of service, like high and consistent levels of parts availability, and providing flexible and dependable delivery services.'

At Ford, Ronald E. Goldsberry, Vice President and General Manager of the Customer Service Division, emphasizes his company's born-again embrace of the customer:

> Our people were proud that they sold parts, just like the vehicle divisions took pride in selling cars. We were sales-oriented. Our field people would ask themselves, 'How many parts did I get?' We have to sell parts, but what was missing was, 'Are

the customers and dealers satisfied? Will what we're doing make the overall company successful?' That should be our primary purpose.

DEALERSHIP DESIGN INCREASINGLY EMPHASIZES SERVICE IMPORTANCE

Acting so that it will benefit from the great importance of the service contact, GM's Saturn Corporation adds a customer-pleasing feature in the way it organizes the dealership layout. Unlike other dealers, which put the showroom in front and hide the service around the back or down a dirty side street, GM's Saturn dealerships proudly place the service entrance at the front. The single reception area at the front of the dealership serves both sales and service.

The Saturn idea is to make the customer feel that the dealer is as concerned about service as they are about sales. This is a very positive approach since, as Honda says, the service contact by the customer is an extremely important opinion-former when they enter and leave the dealership.

PEOPLE WANT SERVICE TO BE CONVENIENT

The siting of service facilities is an important issue, especially as it is expressed in the franchise agreement. Most car manufacturers insist

Fig. 7.1 The Saturn dealerships broke with industry tradition by having the service entrance at the front, to stress the importance of the service contact with the customer.

that service workshops should be housed within the dealership premises. However, there are good reasons why this requirement should be re-examined to the potential benefit of both dealer and customer.

If newer forms of retailing do in fact result in multi-marque 'car barns' or regional auto-parks, they may be sited in areas where the cost of adding service facilities would be too high. The placing of such a facility may also be inconvenient to customers.

Research confirms that car owners prefer to have after-sales service located near to their homes or businesses. In the UK the 1993 Lex Report on Motoring found that 53% of car owners would set a limit of six miles or less on the distance that they would drive to have their car serviced. Only 13% said that they would be willing to drive more than 18 miles. On average, new-car drivers were prepared to travel 11.8 miles and used-car drivers 8.5 miles.

SPLITTING SERVICE FROM SALES SHOULD BE CONSIDERED

People are accustomed by their experience over many years to having sales and service linked in one dealership. Three quarters of Britons who had recently bought a new car told the Lex Report that they thought it was very or fairly important to have the service facility very near to or on the same site as the showroom.

However, strictly from an after-sales service standpoint we do not consider it essential that single-point dealerships offering all services must remain the sole format for car franchising. As with selling, so too with servicing a number of different formats may be developed.

For routine service, mobile teams could come to the home or office to service the car. Cars could be picked up from the owner and taken to service locations which he or she may never see. A dealer can have service reception only, cars being taken to central or subcontract facilities to have specific jobs done. This would allow increasingly costly servicing equipment to be amortized over multiple vehicle makes.

FORD TESTING SATELLITE SERVICE FACILITIES

In Europe Ford is testing a form of satellite service to try to bring the service activity closer to the customer. Ford's concept is that service facilities will be established as satellites to a main dealer, which will be responsible for their operation. Tests of satellite service facilities have been conducted by Ford in Norway and in the UK. Ford's aim is to phase in such a system gradually, taking advantage of changes in its dealer structure, rather than to oblige its installation.

Such satellite arrangements are also being tested in North America. They are positioned in areas very accessible to customers and they keep longer hours than is possible at a normal dealership. Initial customer-satisfaction levels achieved by such satellite service operations are 'very good', says Ford.

CAR OWNERS ARE TAKING THE INITIATIVE

That drivers are already exercising more initiative in their choice of service is indicated by the Lex Report findings. According to *Sewells* [73], 'There has been a drift away from main-dealer servicing towards other methods – friends/acquaintances in particular. It was also evident that the number of drivers giving multiple answers had increased, suggesting that more are using a combination of service providers.'

The Lex findings also underscore the importance of having service activities franchised and monitored by the car makers. The overall rating of the Lex respondents who were 'very satisfied' with the way their cars were serviced was 47%. This rose to 56% when the car was serviced by a dealer representing that specific make.

Customers need to make known their servicing needs – and workshops need to learn how to listen. Columnist Dave Barry discussed these requirements as follows:

> Is there any way that you, the lowly consumer, can gain the serious attention of a large and powerful business? I am pleased to report that there IS a way. According to an Associated Press news report from Russia, an electric company got into a billing dispute with a customer and cut off the customer's electricity. This customer, however, happened to be a Russian Army arsenal. So the commander ordered a tank to drive over to the electric company's office and aim its gun at the windows. The electricity was turned right back on.

One hopes that most customers will not need to go to such lengths to communicate with their service and product providers. Their ability to do so, however, will depend upon the receptiveness of businesses to customer complaints. Much greater receptiveness is required. And in the auto repair business the first line of reception is the service advisor or writer.

SERVICE ADVISOR A KEY POINT OF CONTACT

One of Honda's three important contacts is with the service writer or advisor. 'Many more women are becoming service advisors,' says Keith Magee of Lincoln-Mercury. 'They make excellent service advisors. They are very good at listening to customers and their complaints. A service advisor must listen very well.'

That the sex of the service advisor is not necessarily a positive factor was reported by journalist Stuart Marshall [74]:

Some years ago, I changed the make of our family car mainly because the girl receptionist at the local servicing dealer went out of her way to irritate mature women customers, my wife included. She must have cost that franchise dealer a lot of business.

One former customer switched to Honda. Two days after taking delivery of her Civic, a bouquet and a 'call us any time you need us' letter arrived from the dealer. She will never buy anything but a Honda again. In my experience, the treatment a car owner receives from a franchised dealer can range from excellent to appalling. The best defence against the wrong 'uns is to vote with your feet.

And if a car owner votes with their feet, the dealer will never know why they never returned. It may have taken that dealer quite a while to catch on to the way their service receptionist was treating customers. For this reason dealers must do their utmost to maintain a strong and productive dialogue with their past, present and potential customers.

COMMISSION COMPENSATION OF SERVICE ADVISORS IS COUNTERPRODUCTIVE

Service advisors' actions tend to be coloured by the fact that they are compensated in significant part by commissions on the sales they write. This system is seen as being inherently unsound and anti-consumer by virtually all observers of the automotive retail scene. It needs review and revision.

In the early 1990s one of America's biggest retailers, Sears Roebuck & Company, introduced commissions for service sales staff in many of their Sears Automotive Centers throughout the USA. They also introduced quotas and targets for sales. In 1991, as court cases have subsequently shown, these policies led to heavy abuses that backfired badly on the business and reputation of Sears.

After receiving widespread complaints and lawsuits and triggering a US government enquiry, Sears abandoned the use of commission incentives for service sales staff. This experience vividly dramatizes the risks that car dealers are running by continuing such practices in their service operations.

Successful Texas dealer Carl Sewell disagrees, however. He holds that compensation *entirely* by commission creates a sense of partnership and ensures that his people will act in a customer-friendly way so that clients will return for new cars and service. We do not reject the idea that such a comprehensive application of the commission system could, in conjunction with other management actions, help customer satisfaction. But we do not see it as working well in isolation.

SERVICE TECHNICIANS
MUST UNDERSTAND THE PROBLEM

In addition to the problem of compensation of the service writer or advisor, the difficulty arises that communication between them and the technicians who actually do the work can be poor. This can lead to serious service failures since customers are often barred from speaking directly to the technicians who work on their cars. Correctly understanding and interpreting customer needs is vital to successful repairs.

'Customers are always in a hurry,' writes dealer Carl Sewell [63], 'but we tell them that if they'll just spend an extra ten minutes explaining what's wrong, our chances of fixing it are at least doubled. When we put it that way, customers are willing to take the time.' Nor are all service advisors trained in the art of listening to customers, as they must be, to get them to explain the fault fully and clearly.

To improve both reception and diagnosis, British Ford has arranged for customers to drive their cars directly into a designated reception bay where they can be met by a member of the service team. This allows the customer and technician to meet next to the vehicle to diagnose the work required properly and to carry out other visual checks of the car as needed.

However this is achieved, this is an essential element of the service-writing experience. Only if the car is present when the service receptionist is briefed will it be possible for the customer to point out all those factors with which they may be concerned. The Ford method is one way of accomplishing this; others may well be possible, without the appointment system required by Ford.

IS THE SERVICE ADVISOR OBSOLETE?

We must also question the concept of having a service advisor (actually a salesperson in disguise) as an intermediary between the customer and the technician. 'Customers want direct contact with the technician who repairs their car,' says Sir Trevor Chinn, Chairman and CEO of Lex Service plc, based on his company's surveys of British motorists.

'It is interesting,' continues Chinn, 'that in our chain of non-franchised service centres our research shows a high level of customer satisfaction and repeat business, higher than that generally achieved in dealerships. These satisfaction levels are produced in a very low-cost environment with minuscule levels of supervisory staff and the customers talking directly to the mechanics.'

VIEWING AREA EXPRESSES PRIDE IN FINE SERVICE

Lexus addresses the service contact issue in its dealership design. The Lexus diagnostic service centre has a window looking into one or two service bays. This allows the customer to watch the vehicle being worked on and talk directly with the technician. 'People like watching other people work,' says Carl Sewell [63]. 'This contributes to a sense of theatre. Plus, the window tells customers we're proud of our facilities and the work we do.'

One of the workshops top-rated for customer satisfaction in Germany, the Toyota Autohaus Saxe at Leipzig, has a walkway at mezzanine level around one wall of the service shop. This gives customers an opportunity to see how clean and well-organized the shop is. This is a very strong confidence-building factor. Fully 70% of customers say they would like to have an opportunity to see what's happening when their car is repaired.

These measures, however, must be seen for what they are: a poor substitute for putting the customer in direct contact with the service technician. That is what they would prefer, and they are right to prefer it, because they know that only the technician can inform them clearly about the problem and its solution. Would you prefer to deal with your doctor through a 'medical advisor' who is paid by commission? Enough said.

THE CUSTOMER'S TIME IS VALUABLE TOO

Dealers who are on top of their game are aware of the fact that their customers are busy people whose time is valuable – all the more so by implication if they are driving a more expensive car. If a car has been brought in for a minor service matter, it may be possible to fix it while the customer waits. More and more good dealers are geared up to do this.

This presumes that an attractive place to wait has been arranged, with refreshments readily available. It also presumes that the service department is willing to achieve a customer-satisfying fast turnaround and that it knows well the procedures for making a quick repair correctly the first time.

How fast can good repairs be made? We are certainly not talking about hours. Only minutes can be considered for a while-you-wait repair or installation. Are seconds too ambitious? The Grand Prix teams certainly don't think so. They can change all four tyres and wheels and wipe the windscreen (when there is one) in less than five seconds. That's how a quick repair should be seen: as a fast, safe, efficient pit stop. And if it's not completed in a specified time the customer gets a free stop watch!

Fig. 7.2 For while-you-wait service there is only one standard for best performance: the few seconds needed for a Grand Prix pit stop: here Damon Hill's Williams-Renault in Hungary. *Source:* Empics Ltd, Nottingham.

MORE CONVENIENT SERVICE-SHOP HOURS CAN BUILD BUSINESS

In some countries, such as Germany, limitations on the hours that may be worked have made it difficult to provide a service outside the five weekdays. Nevertheless surveys of drivers consistently show that they would be more likely to bring a car in for service if they could do so on a Saturday.

Most significantly, the interest in taking advantage of Saturday service is particularly strong among those drivers who say that they usually carry out repairs themselves or have them made by friends. These are the customers that car makers are eager to obtain or retain; Saturday working in the workshop appears to be one way to attract them.

One solution to the problem of working hours may well be to exchange Saturday work by technicians and staff for time off on a relatively quiet weekday afternoon. This would help give dealerships the flexibility they need to cope with the changing lifestyles of their customers.

SERVICE NEEDS ACCESS TO CAR'S HISTORY

Service can be improved if the dealer confronted with the car knows its history. This is being assisted in several ways. For example, Saturn dealers take note of the VIN number of the car. By typing it into their computer they are able to see the car's service record at any dealership throughout the USA.

Innovation seems possible in this area. For example, a car could carry with it a 'smart card' that would hold the service history and be readily readable by any dealer for that marque. Also valuable would be a system that used a scanner pen to read the bar-coded VIN number now provided at the base of the windscreen on many cars.

The radio-interrogated computer-chip tags mentioned in Chapter 5 could also play an important role. As Al Fleming noted [44], 'Radio frequency identification tags can track cars and trucks in dealer and fleet inventories and provide instant access to warranty and service data. When tags are tied to a vehicle's on-board computer and diagnostic sensors, pre-warranty conditions can be analysed and corrected *before* product failures occur.'

SUCCESSFUL FIRST-TIME REPAIR IS ESSENTIAL

Most important is ensuring that service work is done right the first time. From its focus groups of owners and its monitoring of all repair orders and complaints registered by its 25 'listening-post' dealers, GM's Cadillac Division has discovered that its customers are most unhappy when their dealer is unable to repair their cars correctly the first time. While over 40% of repairs by all automobile dealers have to be redone, Cadillac told writer Bro Uttal [75], its dealers have lowered their proportion to 35% 'and are still pushing'.

And if a second attempt must be made, says customer satisfaction expert David Freemantle [76], 'Immediate action must be taken, without hesitation, to redress any product defect or shortfall in service to the customer. What is intolerable is the "second order" failure to make swift reparation for a "first order" mistake. Most of us will tolerate the mistake if it is openly and honestly admitted and early action is taken to redress it. *There are no minor problems of customer service.*'

THE MORE SATISFYING THE CAR, THE GREATER
THE DISAPPOINTMENT OVER POOR SERVICE

Also important is the need to avoid creating problems where none exist. Then, when created, they must be dealt with promptly. In *Automotive News* Jack Keebler gives anecdotal evidence of how *not* to proceed [77]:

> Roughly two years ago, I recommended a Ford Taurus SHO to a friend of mine. Just before Christmas, he called to tell me that his beloved Taurus had been called into the dealership for a 'factory

Fig. 7.3 When a person loves a car, as Jack Keebler's friend did his Yamaha-powered Ford Taurus SHO, nothing hurts more than having it perform worse instead of better after service.

recall' on the clutch. He told me he was nervous about taking the car in because he wasn't having any clutch or transaxle-related problems. In a sense, the car wasn't broken so he was reluctant to take it in to get it 'fixed'. His instincts were right on.

When he got the SHO back, the shift lever could not be pushed into the gate without grinding the gear. He immediately went back to the dealership to complain to the service writer. The writer came out to try the transaxle. Although he acknowledged that the shifting was stiff, the horrible grinding sound didn't stop him from attempting to jam the lever into a drive gear.

The dealership kept the car for two days and then returned it to my friend. When the car was picked up the second time, it was warmed up. Gear engagement was not as smooth as it was before 'the service'. But it was significantly better than the first time he got the car back. But imagine my friend's chagrin the next morning when the cold transaxle was just as reluctant to go into gear as it had been the first time he'd picked up the car.

The buddy refuses to take his Taurus back to the dealership that rendered his car undriveable. So since just before Christmas, the unshiftable SHO has sat in his garage under a car cover while he's attempted to resolve his problems through correspondence with various Ford zone officials.

'It takes more than great cars to win and keep this type of customer,' Keebler summarizes. 'It takes great service. And this, obviously, ain't it.' In this case the owner's disappointment in the service was all the greater because he so loved his Yamaha-engined Taurus SHO.

DEALERS NEED LATITUDE
TO AUTHORIZE HELP FOR CUSTOMERS

The SHO anecdote is vivid evidence of the problems that can arise in the satisfaction of customers through the complex relationship that links manufacturer, dealer and customer. Traditionally dealers are not allowed to make special financial adjustments or carry out repairs on cars that are out of the warranty period without charging the customer unless they have received prior factory approval. This can make it very difficult for dealers to act promptly to solve customer problems.

Ford has given its US dealers the independent authority to make such adjustments on out-of-warranty cars up to five years old or up to 50 000 miles. Since late 1991 Ford dealers have been authorized to make a decision on the spot to spend up to $250 to carry out work to satisfy a customer. The level of authorization could be as high as $2000, depending on the particular dealer.

In 1993 Ford upgraded the programme to double the dealer limit to at least $500. As a new policy, Ford allowed dealers to pay customers up to $150 of the $500 for such expenses as hotels or rental cars related to the problem. 'This allows dealers to make decisions for the customers without coming to the company,' explained Pat Hoye, Field Operations Manager for Ford's Customer Service Division [78].

On his own, a British BMW dealer has adopted a similar approach. Says the General Manager of BMW Altwood [78], 'We just believe that to be successful we have to excel at customer service. We have a "coffer" account against which any employee can authorize expenditure to satisfy a customer in resolving a problem. It means our customers have plenty of car parking outside the service reception area. It means we have a 24-hour reception facility.'

MAJOR RISK:
CREATING VOCAL DISSATISFIED CUSTOMERS

Mark Foucher, Cadillac's Manager of Customer Relations, underlined the huge dangers of creating dissatisfied customers: 'An unhappy customer is a terrorist. The unhappy customer makes a point of telling others about the problem, and some of those listeners spread the word still more. Satisfied customers tell eight to ten others. Dissatisfied customers tell 16 to 20 others. Twenty-five percent of the dissatisfied customers may tell as many as 40 other people.'

'It will not suffice to have customers that are merely satisfied,' adds W. Edwards Deming. 'Customers that are unhappy and some that are merely satisfied switch. Profit comes from repeat customers – those that boast about the product or service.' Cadillac has gone so far as to quantify the benefit. According to Mark Foucher, 'it costs five times as much to gain one conquest customer as it does to retain one existing customer.'

FIRST, YOU APOLOGIZE

How should front-line staff cope with unhappy customers? Especially if they are unhappy because the dealership erred? The first step, says dealer Carl Sewell, is to apologize [63]: 'We have to make a big deal out of being wrong. For one thing, we were wrong. The mistake should not have happened. And for another, the problem – no matter what it is – is a very big deal to the customer.

'Normally a spoken apology will be enough. But if it's a bigger deal,' continued Sewell, 'we might write a note, or call, or even – if the problem warrants it (the salesperson, for example, forgot to pick up the car for service) – send a dozen roses. But whatever we do, the customer has to recognise that we're sincere.'

The most difficult challenge for dealers is the apology for a problem that they know is the fault of the car. This is when the customer hears the most galling line of all: 'Oh, they all do that.' Suddenly the customer is made to feel that they made a terrible choice in selecting this car – and perhaps this dealer as well. This is when dealers must become a positive advocate for the interests of their customer without being openly critical of the car maker. Not all will master this subtle balance.

STAFF NEED SYMPATHETIC LISTENING ABILITY

Author Roger Seng counsels restraint and understanding in coping with a dissatisfied customer [79]:

> Let your customer unburden himself. The customer tacitly accepted your representations of potential benefits, advantages, service and satisfaction when he gave you the order. He placed his trust in you and your company, but now something has gone wrong; he feels deceived, exploited, cheated. And he feels a strong urge to vent his fury on someone. You provide a logical target.
>
> Expect him to voice his anger, and let him do so – without interruption or rebuttal even if he is unreasonable and excessive. Then listen – attentively, sympathetically and with no suggestion of antagonism. Obviously, you'll learn some of the circumstances, but more important you will be helping to set the stage for a rational examination of the problem later when a more reasonable atmosphere inevitably returns. Then begin working toward a solution by first reviewing those aspects of the situation that are still favourable or on which you can both agree.

'Believe it or not,' writes David Freemantle [76], 'it doesn't take much to please most customers. Conversely, it often takes a lot to alienate a customer. Customers are extraordinarily forgiving if not extraordinarily appreciative of any positive attitude displayed by an employee. It is absolutely astounding that so few organizations recognise this and therefore fail to encourage such attitudes.'

One of the most successful independent repair companies in Britain is the Kwik-Fit chain, which has 650 service centres and 3500 staff in the UK and other European countries. It successfully attracts some four million customers per year into its centres for a variety of mileage-related car repairs.

The company's Chairman and CEO, Tom Farmer, considers that 'a complaining customer is the greatest opportunity we have to convert into a loyal – and delighted – customer.' The Kwik-Fit way of dealing with a dissatisfied customer has two important elements. First, listening to the customer's complaint without interruption. Second, guaranteeing a speedy solution to the problem.

CUSTOMERS MUST BE ABLE TO EXPRESS THEIR FEELINGS TO A PERSON

Gruelling though it may be at times, even senior executives must be able and willing to be in contact with customers to hear and act on their complaints first-hand. In many instances only human contact will be profound and satisfying enough to defuse a potential customer explosion.

This was the conclusion of Bob Wiper, Chief Executive of Britain's National Tyres and Auto Care. In each of National's 400 branches a poster asks customers to tell their friends if they're happy with the service they received – or to call Wiper at his office, at home or in his car (providing the telephone numbers) if they're unhappy for any reason.

'Our centres are open seven days a week, therefore I have to be,' said Wiper [80]. By stepping out front he has set an example to his employees and has shown that in the service industry of today and tomorrow the 'don't do as I do, do as I say' ethos is no longer good enough.

SYSTEMS CAN HELP SPEED RESPONSES TO CUSTOMERS

Technology can come to the aid of people whose job it is to respond to, and satisfy, customers. In Britain, Ford set a target of two days from the time a customer contact was received to the time when a reply was generated. However, in 1988 an internal study indicated that the average response time was much longer at five working days.

'The solution,' reported *Automotive Engineer* [81], 'was a system known as ORCHID which was developed as a joint exercise by Ford of Britain and Wang (UK).' ORCHID has reduced response time to less than the targeted two days and has also improved service advisor productivity by over 40%. It operates as follows:

> ORCHID allows all incoming letters to be scanned into the imaging system and electronically routed to a Service Advisor. Depending on the situation, the Advisor can, on their own terminal, access the mainframe technical databases, warranty records, corporate policies and decision-support tools as well as the customer's original correspondence.
>
> In addition to eliminating time spent on paper file handling and information searching, the new system allows Advisors to produce their own replies, either from a library of standard letters or by the creation of a customised letter.

'Other U.K. and European automotive manufacturers are developing similar systems in conjunction with Wang (U.K.) based on the software system called CRIS (Customer Response Information System),' reports *Automotive Engineer*. 'Users of this system state that – as a result – the number of satisfied customers has increased and this has led to greater customer loyalty and reduced customer complaints.'

Using a system called DIALOG, personnel at Saturn's Michigan headquarters can monitor communications on the GM subsidiary's Customer Assistance Network. They can observe the nature of the problems in the field as they are happening and thus generate new ideas that can help their service technicians and dealers.

SYSTEMS CAN ALSO GIVE CUSTOMER DIRECT ACCESS TO CAR MAKER

Cadillac dealer Carl Sewell gave credit to that company's fine customer relations for its ability to bridge a period when its products were not up to the mark. At the heart of this effort is Cadillac's Consumer Relations Centre, set up in 1987. The Centre is staffed 24 hours a day by well-educated young men and women. Their demeanour is cordial, yet direct and businesslike. Numbers manning the Centre vary according to the hour of the day from a peak of 24 to two during the shift from midnight to 7 a.m.

Cadillac makes four toll-free telephone lines available to its customers. One line is for fleet customers. Another is for owners of the Allanté two-seater. The two main lines are for Roadside Assistance. *Automotive News* reported on some of its accomplishments:

> On a holiday weekend, a man threw his jacket in the trunk of his Cadillac and slammed it shut – with the car keys in his jacket

pocket. The car had a trunk-release button, but it wouldn't work with the ignition off. The Roadside Assistance gave step-by-step instructions on hot-wiring the trunk button. The owner retrieved his keys.

The Centre has access to data stored by GM's EDS subsidiary on customers, dealers and individual cars. In December 1992 a technician at a Cadillac dealership called requesting the key codes for a 1987 model. From the time the call was received until the numbers were available, the technician's identity verified and the key codes provided, required a total of two minutes.

Since Cadillac's pioneering initiative, roadside assistance has swept the American industry like wildfire. Ford countered with a similar service for Lincoln; from 1994 free roadside service has been included in the price of every new Ford, Mercury and Lincoln. Lincoln owners are eligible for help up to 50 000 miles and the other brands to 36 000 miles. The free assistance includes the delivery of fuel, tyre changes, towing, battery service and help getting into locked cars.

SERVICE UNDER WARRANTY MUST MEET FIRST-CLASS STANDARDS

Work done by dealers under warranty must give full satisfaction. Though research shows that warranties are not high on lists of motivations to buy cars, well-executed service under warranty can help improve customer/dealer relations.

The Japanese approach to warranties is to under-promise and over-deliver. Although car warranties are technically quite short in Japan, in fact they give virtually complete coverage. This allows both manufacturer and dealer to be seen as 'good guys' who fix the owner's car problems even though they aren't technically obliged to according to the written warranty.

In the USA the auto makers have succeeded in exasperating their customers by putting deductible amounts in the fine print of many warranties. These are part of many new-car warranties and also many extended service plans sold to car owners at additional cost. When after making a claim customers discover that the warranty does not fully cover the cost of the necessary repairs, they see themselves as victims of over-promising and under-delivering.

PLEASING CUSTOMERS IS THE ART OF DELIVERING MORE THAN EXPECTED

Promising less and delivering more is the name of the game of gaining satisfied customers. David Freemantle advises [76], 'customer expectations should frequently be exceeded by the provision of unsolicited little extras. What is pleasurable is when the customer receives something good over and above that expected. One of the most exciting aspects of customer service, therefore, is to discover innovative little ways of pleasing the customer even more.'

'Under-promise and over-deliver' is one of the business maxims of independent service provider John Brookes in Chester, UK. When his Cranebank Garage services a car its owner receives a small gift. One month it was a book on places to visit in the countryside; another month it was a road atlas. And when they open the hood they see a spotless steam-cleaned and lacquered engine bay. 'He can't see that we've changed his engine oil, but he *can* see we've taken care to clean the engine,' Brookes says [82].

'Once we get a customer we never let him go,' Brookes added. Cranebank has set up its own computerized customer databank. Car histories are logged so that service and periodic inspection reminders can be sent at appropriate intervals – in addition to 6000 Christmas cards. Information on special customer needs and desires is also recorded.

John Brookes says this is an extension of the way he would like to be treated himself as a customer [83]. 'It is a psychological approach. We also send questionnaires to customers which prove very useful. Last week a lady rang to say that we have done only eight out of the nine jobs she had wanted doing. We took the car back and cured the remaining problem, so we hope she will now be a staunch customer. She said she wouldn't necessarily have contacted us about it if she hadn't had the follow-up letter.'

Cranebank relies on these personal touches to win customers and keep them coming back. 'We find a lot of car buyers don't want to use franchised dealers for servicing after the first two years,' Mr Brookes said. 'They are perceived as being impersonal and not giving value for money.' This is the challenge facing the franchised outlets: to enhance the personal nature of service contacts and to avoid gouging on service charges.

SATURN GIVES MORE THAN EXPECTED IN MAJOR RECALL

Saturn, one of the world's most customerized auto companies, decided to give much more than expected when it recalled 380 682 cars to fix a problem that had caused some engine fires. Setting a target of completing 90% of the recall within 90 days, Saturn authorized its dealers to spend money to make the experience as pleasant as possible for its owners. 'The attitude we've taken is that it's an opportunity to talk with the customer and demonstrate our commitment,' said Don Hudler of Saturn [84].

Dealers could spend Saturn's money to provide food and refreshments to customers, courtesy cars and transportation and tickets to movies or sports events. If a customer couldn't come in, the dealer was authorized to conduct the recall installation at their home.

In addition to these courtesies dealers hired extra personnel, washed and valeted cars and extended service opening hours during the recall. Some dealers organized 'recall parties' with barbecues on a Saturday to encourage customers to come in.

Realizing that the large-scale recall could arouse concern among its owners, Saturn even wrote to those whose cars were not affected to inform them about the problem and its solution. 'People will hear by word of mouth how we handle customers,' said Saturn's Hudler, 'and they will say if that's how they treat us, we'll buy.' Word of mouth, already one of Saturn's most powerful marketing methods, is being further enhanced by the right actions in adversity.

CAR MAKERS CAN HELP DEALERS DEVELOP CUSTOMER-HANDLING SKILLS

Saturn's dealer policies are unusual. Typically the car industry takes the view that 'a large part of the responsibility for building customer relationships lies with the dealer – after all it is he who establishes and maintains the personal contacts.'

Nevertheless it is clear that the car maker must lead the team for developing and maintaining this customer contact. Dealers are necessarily too wrapped up in their daily business affairs to be expected to see and act on the 'big picture' of car and brand image and reputation.

In the USA, Ford's field personnel work closely with dealers on the improvement of their operating performance. Ford rates its dealers according to eight basic standards. Ford's field people start with two particular standards for a dealer and work with them to improve performance according to those standards within a set time. In the previous chapter we described Chrysler's Customer One programme, developed and implemented with the help of an outside agency, Ross Roy.

In such ways manufacturers can be advisers to dealers in improving customer satisfaction. They can stress the advantages of the use of a database marketing system and other actions by dealers to help strengthen customer contacts. The dealer is the face of the product, but [85] 'the manufacturer must work hard to determine the expression put on that face.'

An example of the desired expression is provided by the previously-mentioned UK BMW dealership. A customer said of it [76]:

> It is very easy to get through on the telephone and get your car booked in for service. Everyone is very polite. On arrival you are shown to a desk. There is rarely any waiting. You are treated as an individual. Coffee is available if you want it. They provide courtesy cars when your car is out of action. They also keep you

constantly involved with the company – inviting you to various events to enjoy the BMW experience. On collecting my car from service, I always find it has been valeted and polished. Everything is over and above what you expect – and more than what you asked for.

ACCOMPANY THE BAD NEWS WITH THE GOOD NEWS

Most people don't know all that much about how their car works. They trust the dealer and the service people to interpret their needs and complaints and act to meet their needs. So how do they know in fact that they are really getting value from their servicing expense? How can that third important Honda contact, at the service-department cashier's desk, be made more constructive? Modern information technology makes it possible.

Every service action must relate in some way to operating factors that the customer can appreciate. Replacing burned-out bulbs enhances safety. Renewed shock absorbers improve ride comfort. An engine oil change adds to longevity. Every check made on a scheduled service list is an action taken to avoid future problems, extend vehicle life and assure driving and riding pleasure. Why not tell all this to the person who pays the bill?

In addition to the usual columns of money spent, a customer-friendly invoice will have another column in which information will automatically be printed about the benefits provided by every service operation. The bigger the numbers at the bottom of the bill, the more this information will be appreciated by customers – and by their personal or business accountants.

The bill for service can perform several other functions. It can, for example, print clearly when the next service should be arranged. In addition it can point out the environmental advantages of the service that was provided. If oil has been changed, for example, it can point to the environmentally-sound disposal of the waste oil used by the workshop.

WOMEN MUST BE MUCH BETTER TREATED

On the service side as well as the sales side of car dealerships women are often treated all too poorly. A German survey of 120 women who drive cars and take care of their servicing revealed some of the attitudes experienced by this important and influential owner body.

By far the biggest reason for dissatisfaction with service in dealerships among women is a fear of being cheated (77%). The feeling that they aren't being taken seriously troubles 62% of women. Fifty-eight per cent believe their questions haven't been answered and 51% find the bill to be too high. Forty-two per cent complain of being addressed in jargon or lacking a suitable discussion partner. A third consider the dealership personnel to be unfriendly.

Regrettably, research has confirmed that women have every reason to worry about being cheated in repair shops. In Britain the same car was taken on different occasions by a man and a woman to various branches of independent repair shops for quotes on the work that needed to be done. Overall, on average the shops told the man that the work would cost £114. The average estimate for the woman was £144, 26% higher [86].

SERVICE CHARACTERISTICS PARTICULARLY DESIRED

Of the desired characteristics of a service operation, women put trustworthiness at the top of their list (92%), just ahead of reliability (88%). Also at the level of more than 80% as requirements are speed and value. Sixty-three per cent are looking for friendly personnel and 51% are hoping that everything will be explained in a proper manner.

From these factors and others the German research drew conclusions about the kind of service that women would like to see in an ideal workshop. Leading their wish list is a personal discussion partner (81%) and firm pricing (80%). Three quarters would like to have the invoice clearer and more illustrative and 65% would like the repairs carried out on the car to be explained. Also valuable, say 71% of the respondents, is a precise 'menu' of the repair services on offer.

Surveys in Germany conflict on the desirability of the provision of a service to pick up and deliver a car for repairs. Overall some 60% of service customers consider that this is desirable. On the other hand only 22% of women judge it to be a feature they would like in their 'ideal dealership'.

At the present state of the art this implies that women judge that they have more free time to bring and collect the car. They may well see it as just another task on their daily travels. On the other hand, dealers should definitely not take for granted that women may not desire this service.

THERE IS NO SUCH THING
AS A SECOND-CLASS CUSTOMER

The German researchers also visited some 25 dealerships to gain a personal impression of the way in which women are dealt with. Their conclusion, said the authors of the study, was that most dealers clearly give themselves the luxury of dealing with women as second-class customers.

Women were particularly critical of the way in which they were spoken to, and of the reliability and trustworthiness of the dealership.

They said [87] that a dealership 'should no longer be a club for men with oil-smeared hands and macho behaviour'.

Special emphasis in their findings was laid on the importance of transparency. This referred to such points as a clear explanation of repairs, unprompted presentation of parts that were changed and a full presentation of the service pricing. The repair note should also carry a remark or two by the technician who carried out the work, together with their name and signature.

THE NEED FOR AN 'ADULT-TO-ADULT' RELATIONSHIP

As in so many aspects of dealership operations, none of these actions would be of special value to women alone. They would in fact be appreciated by all car owners who do business with the service department of a dealer or an independent workshop. What is needed is what has been aptly described as an 'adult-to-adult' relationship.

For example, in Britain in the early 1990s Ford carried out extensive customer surveys to support the introduction of new retailing methods. In the area of service, Ford found, the key customer requirements are: improved reception and diagnosis arrangements, 'no surprises' service pricing and improved customer information – very much the specific requests made by the women interviewed in Germany.

In response, Ford is adopting a national menu-pricing initiative to promise that 'the price you see is the price you pay' for the majority of service and maintenance work.

PROFILING OF SERVICE CUSTOMERS ACCORDING TO NEEDS

Women, like all workshop customers, must be looked after in a more correct and professional way. But this does not mean that customers must be viewed as a bland mass. Rather, they are individuals as regards both their problems and their desires.

'We need to profile and differentiate our customers according to their needs,' says Knut Schüttemeyer, Global Service Co-ordinator for the Volkswagen Group. 'For example separate need-groupings are women, young people, business customers or family customers – each with a different set of requirements. If we can adapt our service performance to such needs groups then we have a profiling of our market according to needs. This is the path we must follow. It no longer holds true that young people only drive old cars or women only second cars.

'The quality of handling customers is not necessarily a question of high investment,' adds Schüttemeyer. 'The customer must have the impression that the staff has grasped his problems on a personal level and is not merely dealing with him on the level of technical problems.'

ENLIGHTENED POLICIES
ACHIEVE MEASURABLE BENEFITS

In the USA, Ford has introduced a number of new policies affecting relations with dealers and customers: the granting of more freedom to deal directly with customer complaints and the equipping of Ford personnel to work pro-actively with dealers to help them upgrade their customer-facing performance.

Helped by this 'combination of old-fashioned value and newfangled dealer relations,' said *Automotive News* in 1993 [88], 'Ford Division is becoming the 800-pound gorilla of automotive marketing. Ford is listening to dealers, who profit from higher sales, higher warranty reimbursement and better support for customers after the sale.' The magazine said in an editorial column:

> Division General Manager Ross Roberts learned a few lessons from Saturn Corporation and set free some of the power of Ford's 4,300 dealers. Essentially, Ford is offering greater value and better customer service than in the past. While reducing cash incentives, Ford offers loaded cars and trucks at the prices people are willing to pay. The economy may have been weak in 1992, but the Division's sales rose 13% and its share of the car and light truck market rose 2.3 points to 20.3%. And the gains continue.

The findings are empirical, to be sure. But Ford's new policy of working constructively with its dealers must get much of the credit for its growing strength in a difficult market against intense import and domestic competition.

MANUFACTURERS ARE SURVEYING
CUSTOMER SATISFACTION

Manufacturers measure all aspects of dealer service performance by opinion surveys that generate a Customer Satisfaction Index (CSI). Although all firms have some type of customer-satisfaction survey, they differ in the way in which they conduct these.

In Germany, for example, Ford conducts a survey two months after purchase and another 24 months after the acquisition of the new car. In the latter case the survey is specifically directed at the satisfaction of customers with the service performance of their dealer.

At Adam Opel AG, on the other hand, a questionnaire is sent six months after the vehicle is purchased. In cases where it is warranted, Opel uses the questionnaires as a means of letting the dealer know that a customer has a particular problem. This allows the dealer to recontact the customer and solve any remaining problems.

An official of J.D. Power, a leading CSI researcher, warned of some of the ways in which dealers seek to play this new game to their own advantage [89]:

For the dealer, customer satisfaction measures can be a hurdle to be passed by means fair or foul. Many companies have sprung up to offer dealers instant solutions, in the form of programmes to mail cookie tins to customers in the hope that they will give a better report to the dealer. Some dealers even offer to 'help' customers fill out the survey questionnaire.

'Manufacturers sometimes do not help the situation by putting all the emphasis on the measure itself, not on the real purpose behind it – improving customer satisfaction,' the Power executive warned. 'Already at many companies the CSI studies have been separated from the marketing research departments, often placed directly in the service area. While this expedites action follow-up from the results, there is a very real danger that CSI becomes yet another new specialism divorced from the central strategic thrust of the company' – which must be the aim of satisfying more customers.

DEALERS ARE REWARDED (BRIBED?) TO SATISFY CUSTOMERS

In Europe as in the USA, the carrot of financial gain is used to encourage improved CSI performance. Renault is an example of an auto company that is using the cash carrot as part of its dramatic transition toward a market-led culture.

Philippe Gamba, Renault's Director of Marketing, says:

> Before, it was our job to sell the cars that were given to us by the engineers; but today it's completely different. Today there is a new culture. We used to say that we built two million cars a year, not that we have two million customers a year.
>
> Before, we measured our dealers' performance only on sales. Now, more and more of his remuneration is based on the quality of his service.

Renault's 60 company-owned dealers, which sell some one in three of Renaults in France, were informed in 1993 that their earnings would depend increasingly on how well they treated their customers.

Some companies hold back a certain percentage of the selling discount to be paid to those dealers performing satisfactorily. Other makers, such as Chrysler in the USA, give a bonus over and above the normal per-car discount to top-performing dealers.

In Chrysler's 'Drive for the Gold' incentive programme a dealer with a poor CSI rating earns nothing. At the highest Gold level a dealership can be awarded as much as $300 per vehicle. 'For a store selling 1000 new vehicles a year,' writes Joseph Bohn [60], 'that's a potential $300 000 in extra money from the factory.' Moving up from the Bronze level of reward to the Silver level can add an average of $10 000 a month or $120 000 a year of incentive money for dealers selling 1000 vehicles.

FINANCIAL PENALTIES CAN AID MOTIVATION, COMMUNICATE DETERMINATION

Auto service providers should consider the policies of the many public-service organizations that compensate customers if service is not timely or correct. In Britain the pioneer of such schemes was East Midland Electricity. Since its launch in 1985 East Midland's compensation scheme has been expanded to cover 16 different service targets.

'Our market research told us that we weren't trusted by our customers,' Nick Akers, East Midland's corporate relations manager, told John Willman [90]. 'We had a reputation of saying we'd come on Wednesday and turning up on Thursday.' Now customers can ask for service calls to be within a two-hour time slot or even at a specific time. If they fail to turn up, the customer pockets £20.

'The scheme certainly appears to have been successful in improving the company's image, giving it higher satisfaction ratings than other utilities in the area,' Willman reported. 'Providing such compensation has been relatively inexpensive. With 99.74% of appointments kept, less than £35 000 was paid out in the nine months to the end of March 1992.'

'It provides an internal discipline for the company itself,' said Nick Akers of East Midland. 'Staff know that they are expected to meet customer service targets, so the company ends up paying out very little.' It's a concept that can have its motor industry applications as well.

PAYING DEALERS FOR HIGH CSI NOT NECESSARILY THE ANSWER

In Germany the results of customer-satisfaction surveys are generally not translated into bonuses or adjustments to the dealer discounts. Ford's German policy was confirmed by Heinz H. Soiron, Deputy Chairman of Ford Werke AG. He stated that no financial support is offered to dealers in connection with their achievement of their customer-satisfaction goals.

Said Mr Soiron, 'We appeal to the commitment of the man in charge to declare customer satisfaction as a top priority. Because the dealer principal must set the example, must be really convinced that this idea is right. If this is the case we assist him with customer-oriented training programmes.'

BMW, however, is an exception. BMW offers an additional discount of 0.5% for dealers who participate in the BMW Customer Report programme. In addition a 'Top Bonus' of 0.5% is provided from the results achieved. Those dealers get the maximum bonus who reach 59% of the average customer-satisfaction level of the 10 best dealers surveyed.

REAL CUSTOMER SATISFACTION
SHOULD REDUCE DEALER SELLING COSTS

Where financial incentives for high CSI methods are most used, in America, they are also most disliked by dealers. A 1992 survey of dealers by the NADA gained responses from 6158 outlets. Fully two thirds of them said that CSI or SSI (Sales Satisfaction Index) scores should not be linked with incentive payments.

Moreover, fairness to dealers should require all of them to buy the same car at the same price in a given market. This suggests that the idea of using a financial incentive to encourage good CSI performance may not be the best solution in the long run.

Our judgement is that CSI ratings and performance bonuses are an example of the wrong way to view the problem – and the opportunity – of top-flight customer service and satisfaction. Although the actions being taken and requested by motor companies today to improve customer satisfaction are seen by them and their dealers as being expensive, they will in fact *reduce* costs if implemented with a real customer focus. This concept is discussed further in Chapter 9.

In the short term, to be sure, there are added costs. More field staff are being brought into action by car makers and their service agencies to train dealers. CSI research is needed to check performance against targets. Dealers are adding staff by hiring customer satisfaction managers to look after and help satisfy customers.

SURVEY SHOWS IMPORTANCE OF
UNDERSTANDING CAR OPERATION

Real benefits can be achieved through a better understanding of the car's service and operating needs, especially by drivers of cars in company fleets. According to a survey conducted by National Breakdown in the UK, the main cause of breakdowns in company-owned cars is the failure of their drivers to carry out even basic servicing [91]. Even when warning lights come on they usually ignore them!

Improved customer-friendly indoctrination on the features and operation of a new car will significantly increase reliability. This must enhance satisfaction and lead to an early positive decision to buy again from the same dealer and same car maker.

Says Lincoln–Mercury's Keith Magee, 'We encourage dealers to take customers into the service area when they come in to purchase a car and introduce them to the service advisor so they understand the process when they come in for service. That will help them feel very confident about coming back to the dealership for service.' It will also help the owner to have access to information about their car.

CAR ITSELF COULD INSTRUCT THE OWNER

How realistic is it to expect dealer staff to carry out owner briefings? Is this an area where the car maker should help? Infested with legal jargon, owner's manuals are often unreadable. They could be better. Even better, the car maker could bring computer power to the party.

With a built-in memory chip, a car could have a tutorial instrument panel. It would be analogous to the 'help' systems of computer programs which assist the operator in understanding the way the program works.

With a tutorial instrument panel the various controls would be cycled through a routine that uses both sound and light information to tell and show the owner which controls are performing what functions and how they work. It would be a built-in feature of the car that could be activated at any time to instruct a driver new to the vehicle.

ACTIONS BY CAR MAKERS CAN BE HELPFUL

The Japanese auto makers have been leading the way worldwide towards the use of fewer direct suppliers to their production lines. In Japan a major producer may have only 300 or fewer final suppliers, instead of 1000 or more as in Europe or America. With fewer first-tier suppliers Toyota, for example, can check the number of a part in the USA and rapidly find out where, when and by whom the part or assembly was made in Japan. Nissan in the UK has a similar capability.

This system has several benefits. When a recall is necessary, the offending supplier can quickly be identified and alerted. It is also very helpful in tracking down any product faults identified from field information on warranty or other service requirements.

The car makers also have an obligation to build cars that are serviceable. When car columnist Lesley Hazleton worked in a service shop she cursed the Renault designer who had inaccessibly positioned an emergency-brake cable. On the other hand, she writes [92], 'when we put a Mazda up on the lift one day and I saw the oil filter right there within easy reach, I was astonished. Few cars are designed with repairs in mind.'

MANAGE BY DISRUPTION
TO SATISFY THE CUSTOMER

Bill Boggs, a Honda dealer in San Francisco, has introduced a series of measures to attract and hold customers that he calls 'Turning his dealership on its head – management by disruption.' Some of the methods Mr Boggs uses are as follows:

- Cars can be brought in for service or repairs without a prior booking. Every effort is made to complete repairs the same day but 30 loan cars are also available.
- For fitting such small items as antennas, antifreeze, floor mats and wiper blades (items that customers could take care of themselves if they wished to) no labour charges are made.
- A viewing gallery is provided so that customers can see what is happening in the service department.
- Customers can accumulate points for their purchases that can be redeemed for various services and accessories provided by the dealership.
- To keep customers from going to specialized fast-fit and tyre sellers, a dedicated tyre-fitting bay is near the service reception area, providing tyres and fitting at virtual cost price. The objective of this is to keep customers from going to fast-fit outlets and thus ultimately losing their business.
- A fast oil-change service is provided, branded independently as 'Castrol'. This is seen as a tool to attract older cars to the dealership and keep them coming back in the future.

Note that these measures are seen as part of an overall effort to improve teamwork in and throughout the Boggs Honda dealership. In many respects they are as valuable in helping internal communication to assist a team spirit as they are externally as customer-facing measures. Real teamwork with the customer's needs in view: that's how to provide customer-pleasing service.

POINTS FOR DISCUSSION AND REVIEW

- Why should customers be encouraged to complain about problems with their car or servicing?
- Who does Honda identify as the most important customer contacts with a dealer, and why?
- Discuss the positive and negative aspects of the compensation of service advisors by commission.
- What can the Grand Prix Formula 1 teams teach a dealer's service workshop?
- Why does Cadillac consider that an unhappy customer is a 'terrorist'?
- List and discuss three important ways of dealing with a dissatisfied customer.
- What do we mean by 'accompany the bad news with the good news'?

Customer-driven car-owner communications 8

The communications activities of car maker, distributors and dealers provide an umbrella over all their functions as described in the previous chapters. How they communicate both with customers and with their own organization will determine how customer-pleasing their operations will be.

As in other customer interfaces, under-promising and over-delivering should be the watchword of effective communications. In the car industry, unfortunately, the reverse is more common. In this chapter we discuss communications and media relations.

COMMUNICATIONS MUST AMPLIFY AND ENRICH CUSTOMER CONTACTS

One of the industry's best-informed observers is Keith Crain, publisher of *Automotive News*. In a 1993 column he described for his readers the importance of strong, convincing communications with car owners who are experiencing the many influences that will lead to their next purchase decision.

'It's essential for the customer to have a continually pleasant experience with the brand and the model and the dealer and the sales staff and the service department and the manufacturer,' Crain wrote [93]. 'You can't wait until the buying cycle starts all over.'

He further commented:

> Today you must keep in close touch with the customer and develop a relationship that not only begins before the sale but continues throughout the period of ownership. Too often in the car business we wait for the repurchase, hoping that the ownership experience was pleasant. We don't worry about what we can do during the time of ownership to improve the customer's feeling about the products.
>
> Well, that's all changing. Keeping the customer is going to become all-important. Replacing the customer will become increasingly expensive. Companies will spend more and more money on

owners, to make sure that they remain in the fold. The relationship between manufacturer, dealer and vehicle owner is going to change. It will become a real relationship, rather than just an occasion. Understand, join up, or watch out.

WHOSE CUSTOMER IS IT ANYWAY?

Few issues in the relationship between car makers and their dealers are more controversial than communications. To whom does the end customer 'belong'? Who should be communicating with them? Who should pay for which communications to the customer? The issues extend all the way from co-operative advertising to information brochures, house magazines and direct-mail marketing.

One answer is clear: in this age of information and cheap database power there is no reason why a dealer of virtually any size should not have and use a coded list of past, present and potential customers to help maintain regular contacts. Like other aspects of customer satisfaction, as discussed earlier, this must be seen as a cost which will more than repay itself in added profitability for the dealer. This may be an area in which dealer groups will have an advantage, since they can centralize such functions.

Thus car-maker planning must proceed on the assumption that dealers will have and be able to use such databases. The presumption by all parties must be that dealers will use their databases for their own immediate benefit in such a way as to keep customers satisfied with their way of doing business, irrespective of the brand they represent. Thus car makers should not count on dealers to use their databases to do work for them – unless they pay dealers for their assistance as they would any other external marketing service.

COMMUNICATIONS MUST SUPPORT
STRONG, DISTINCTIVE BRAND POSITIONING

So what is there left for the car maker to communicate? They have, after all, a tremendously important job. Their task is to define, develop and deliver a convincing brand positioning statement. Only the car maker is in a position to perform this vital task in all the world markets in which they are active.

The need for stronger brand statements and arguments is acute. More crowded markets and more intense competition mean that car makers must try harder than ever to communicate their brand-positioning arguments to both present and potential customers.

' "OK" products aren't OK any more,' stressed Laurel Cutler, vice chairman of advertising agency FCB/Leber Katz Partners and a former senior Chrysler marketing executive [94]. 'But *great* products, at both ends of the spectrum, will make their makers, and their distributors, very rich. There is no future for products everybody likes "a little," only for products somebody likes a lot. Put another way: going for the "middle-of-the-road" in the 1990s is a sure way to wind up in the ditch.'

'One other thing about brands,' added Cutler, 'especially automotive brands. Cars and trucks must be built and branded for people who are reaching. Consumer aspirations always reach upward, never down – always outward, never inward.'

CHALLENGES TO CLEAR BRAND POSITIONING

The brand-positioning challenge is already massive in the USA, where all auto makers have been struggling for nearly a decade to respond to the buyers' market of the 1990s. In a buyers' market, brand images can take a terrible beating because advertising tends to be deal-related rather than brand-related. Car makers must resist this trend. Re-establishing (or in many cases simply establishing) 'brand salience' in all world markets must be a top priority for car producers.

Brand-communication problems are being intensified in the motor industry by the sharing of products between branded manufacturers. The introduction into the Honda network in the USA of the Isuzu-built Passport 4×4 sport-utility is an example (see page 54).

The owner of a Honda/Isuzu dealership was in the vanguard in this situation: 'There are a lot of joint-venture products out there, and we have to explain that to customers. The Passport is still backed by the Honda factory, so to me it's a Honda product.'

Another Honda/Isuzu dealer says that he is successfully selling his Passports even though they cost slightly more than the same vehicle presented as the Isuzu Rodeo: 'It's pretty strange, but loyal Honda buyers want that Honda name tag, even if they know it's really an Isuzu.' That's brand salience working to the benefit of Honda.

STRONG BRAND SALIENCE HELPS BUILD 'VIRTUAL WALLS' IN SHOWROOMS

The impact of effective brand communications is identifiable at the point of sale. As discussed earlier, many people do come into the showroom with a brand, product and even model preference already established. In the USA, Ford and Nissan jointly produce a minivan which each sells, with only slight appearance differences, respectively as the Mercury Villager and Nissan Quest. There is no difference in the product content.

So what happens in dealerships where both are sold? Dealers who have both Mercury and Nissan franchises told Arlena Sawyers of *Automotive News* that people are not easily swayed from the brand that they sought when they came in: 'People generally come looking

Fig. 8.1 Identical though they are in virtually all respects, the Nissan Quest (left) and Mercury Villager (right) each have strong adherents who place their trust in the Nissan or the Mercury brand – even when both are in the same showroom.

for one or the other,' said Tim North, president of John North Lincoln-Mercury-Nissan in Emporia, Kansas [95]. 'If they're looking for a Villager in a certain colour or trim and we don't have it, they don't say, "How about a Quest?" *We* have to say that.'

Mike Billingsley, an owner of Billingsley Ford-Lincoln-Mercury-Nissan in Ardmore, Oklahoma, added: 'Customers are responding to an image on advertising. We don't try to switch them; we find it easier to show them what they came to see.'

Could this result be reassuring to Europe's car makers who are deeply nervous about several brands sharing a showroom? We believe it should be – as long as they have done an effective job of brand communication and reinforcement. Strong brands, well communicated, can create 'virtual walls' within showrooms as the Passport/Rodeo and Villager/Quest examples demonstrate.

ADVERTISING CLIENTS MUST DISCIPLINE THE COMMUNICATIONS SYSTEM

With the theme established and the target consumer groups identified, how are the messages best conveyed? Advertising pioneers in Europe are still struggling to find the best pan-European media among the still-dominant national newspapers and magazines, with terrestrial television important in only a few cases.

Communication effectiveness across Europe is a gamble with high-cost stakes. It demands clear policy definition, tight guidelines and emphatic leadership. However, car makers are exhibiting little discipline in defining and executing their brand programmes for Europe as a whole. A common agency structure for Europe is rarely available even to the largest companies.

A single pan-European agency structure would make sense, as would centralized advertising creativity and production. It is not essential, though, if clients themselves are able to steer a coherent programme.

INCREASED CLIENT PROFESSIONALISM NEEDED

Surprisingly, according to auto-company advertising agencies, it is their clients who have the least-effectively-organized European communications structures. Clients need to make sure that their own internal systems are working properly before asking their agencies for help.

One reason for lack of coordination on the client side is that it is unusual for auto companies to have advertising professionals responsible for their advertising. Advertising executives in the auto companies have often come up through sales or some other avenue and are rarely professionals trained or experienced in advertising.

Car advertising must be an effective blend of high-level brand reinforcement with regional tactical campaigns. Needless to say this is a combination of demands that does require real professionalism. Dealers in particular will call more and more for increased regional emphasis. They are justified in doing so, because regional advertising strongly reinforces both the product and marketing communications according to local circumstances.

SOUND BUSINESS POLICIES CAN HAVE HUGE ADVERTISING BENEFITS

The Saturn policy of selling its cars according to firm prices throughout its dealer network has important benefits to its advertising policy. For example, Saturn is able to spend its television budget on advertisements which speak about the merits of the vehicle and the pleasurable ownership experience instead of deal after deal.

All too often Saturn's rivals in the marketplace are using their valuable television time to push special offers, rebates and price propositions. This hardly benefits the long-term perception of the customer concerning the merits of the product and service experience. In fact it is almost certainly counterproductive in brand salience terms.

Saturn believes strongly in drawing examples from real-life owners of Saturns, a concept which communicates well in both television and print advertising. Ron Zarrella, GM Vice President and Group Executive for Sales, Service and Marketing, complimented Saturn on advertising that is so distinctive and, at the same time, so consistent that it can be identified as 'Saturn' even if the brand isn't mentioned.

Unlike most other companies, Saturn keeps a number of advertisements in circulation simultaneously. For example, seven or eight print ads and a similar number of television spots could be in use at any one time. Saturn decides the length of time these ads will be used according to their effectiveness. Some might disappear after six to twelve months while others could remain in use for up to two years.

MARKETERS MUST FEEL AND TASTE
THE MARKETPLACE

Marketing must inform customers that they will gain greater satisfaction from dealing with the company and its products. This must have grass-roots impact.

Anita Roddick of the successful Body Shop store chain stresses the need for a practical approach [96]: 'I have heard of no marketing giants or consultants that spend more time on the selling floor, meeting customers, understanding the merchandise, watching the sales people, plugging into the customer and asking "Are you satisfied? Have the merchandise and service met your expectations?" '

In sales as well as in car R&D and design, Roddick stresses the need in communications and marketing to be on the scene and in touch with real live customers. 'I know that the word "marketing" usually means an excuse for gathering around the table to talk,' Roddick adds. 'To talk on and on around every function other than the most important function which is selling the product, understanding the product and valuing the product.'

SPECIAL DISPLAY FACILITIES
SERVE CAR-MAKER BRANDING NEEDS

The need for direct communication with present and potential customers is served by the special display centres established by the Japanese makers in Tokyo and now (by Toyota) in Osaka. By displaying both current models and concept vehicles in settings reflecting the past and the future they create a 'theme centre' atmosphere that makes them an attractive destination for families and young people.

In a special theatre using banks of high-definition monitors, visitors to Toyota's new Osaka centre can watch the production stages of the company's cars. Cars are not sold there, a company spokesman stressed, for the centre is intended to 'subtly draw consumers into the Toyota net, leaving the nuts and bolts of sales to conventional dealers'.

The sales side is not overlooked, however. Trained advisors guide the visitors through the Toyota range and make sure that they know how to find their nearest dealer. With a computerized system that is wired into dealerships, specific new and used cars can be located in the company inventory throughout Japan. As a total statement of the skill and commitment of a car company, such centres communicate powerfully.

CUSTOMER TARGETING ESSENTIAL TO GOOD COMMUNICATIONS

Communication can only be effective if the target customers are clearly identified. In 1987 a research team from the University of Warwick carried out a study of a closely-matched sample of 45 British, US and Japanese companies competing in four markets in the UK: hi-fi, machine tools, household electrical goods and office equipment.

'Segmentation and positioning are at the heart of modern marketing,' the study pointed out. 'It was therefore alarming to discover that 47% of British and 40% of the U.S. companies (versus 13% of the Japanese) acknowledged that they were unclear about the main types of customers in the markets and what their needs were.'

The marketing director of a British company told the researchers, 'I don't know if we segment the market or how we really position ourselves against the competition, but I expect our advertising agency knows ... I think we are probably upmarket because we advertise in some very posh magazines.'

Japanese companies were found to have the clearest view of their existing and potential customers and of how to reach them. They were found to concentrate their marketing investments on high-potential groups.

COMPANY-BACKED PERIODICALS MUST BE MORE TARGETED

Targeting has implications for the car industry in many areas. In 1993, for example, both Chevrolet and Ford ceased publishing 'house magazines' dedicated to their brands. *Ford Times* in particular was an institution in its own right and apparently a valid means of reaching Ford owners between purchases. Was Ford wrong to drop it?

In the era of targeted marketing, it was the right decision. So broad is the Ford product range, let alone Mercury and Lincoln as well, that no single publication could appeal strongly to all owners. It would have much more impact if Ford were to design and promote publications appealing to the owners of specific models. Some unsolicited title suggestions are *Continental Lifestyle*, *Mustang Country*, *Taurus Times* and *Explorer Quarterly*.

Targeted communications should appeal strongly to particular owner groups. In the USA, for example, Isuzu has a dedicated Owner Communications Programme which focuses on the needs and interests of its owners. As part of the programme all letters received by Isuzu from its customers are answered by its senior executives.

Isuzu launched the programme after realizing in 1992 that a third of the initial sales of its redesigned Trooper sport-utility were to owners of older Troopers. This sensitized Isuzu to the need to maintain effective contact with its current owner body. Said an Isuzu executive, 'We recognised that relationship marketing and our loyal owners were an issue we wanted to address. Conquest sales are five times as expensive as sales to loyal owners.'

THE LEXUS COMMUNICATION: TARGETED MARKET AND THE RIGHT MESSAGE

There are many good examples of targeted marketing. One programme Lexus undertook in the USA is particularly instructive. Lexus dealers participating in the programme offered a free oil change to owners of particular Mercedes-Benz and BMW models – clearly-identifiable target customers. While the oil was being changed, a Lexus was loaned to the owner.

When the owner returned to pick up his or her car it had also been washed and valeted and an appropriate gift had been left on the passenger's seat. This provided a persuasive indication of the customer-friendly way in which Lexus started and in which it intended to continue.

CADILLAC'S TARGETED AND PERSONALIZED ROAD SHOW

GM's Cadillac Division is taking its communications activity directly to current and prospective customers. Cadillac's objective is to cater to the new generation of buyers who wish to be more informed before purchase and have a more sophisticated knowledge of automobile features and technology.

In each city it visits, Cadillac invites 10 000 Cadillac owners and 10 000 owners of competitive models. In participation it averages 1000 participants per city, a third of whom are driving competitive models. Cadillac stresses to potential participants that its regional presentations are conducted without salespeople. Cadillac's aim is to provide information without pressure.

After a 40-minute product presentation the visitors are able to ride and drive Cadillac cars on a closed-track environment, usually in a stadium parking lot. In separate sessions focusing on performance and safety the participants can drive four or five Cadillac models. Included is a demonstration of the effectiveness of anti-lock braking.

Session participants are given a coupon for a compact-disc unit or chrome wheels, either of which will be provided on a Cadillac purchased before certain dates. After the session Cadillac sends a questionnaire to all participants. If their response indicates that they would like to consider a purchase, only then is a sales approach made.

These customer presentations were inspired by a tour of Cadillac's zone offices conducted by the GM Division to inform its own people about its new cars and their performance against competitors. Said Cadillac's Manager of Incentive Programmes, David Fitzwalter, 'We saw the excitement generated with the sales people. We wondered if there was a new way of getting to our customers and having this much excitement.'

PERSONAL COMMUNICATIONS ARE THE MOST MEMORABLE

An organization's people are its ideal communications medium. All practitioners of first-class customer service stress that it must be delivered personally. W. Edwards Deming emphasized this to the organizations he advised [14]:

> Everyone, whether he sees the customer or not, has a chance to build quality into the product or into the service offered. The people that see the customers are the marketing department. Do they know it? Does the management teach drivers that they are not only drivers, but a potential influence to increase patronage? How about screening applicants for their adaptability to this role?
>
> A driver, as he descends the stairs to take charge of his truck in the Baltimore terminal of Roadway Express, sees himself in a full-length mirror with this caption: 'You are looking at the only person in our company that our customers ever see.' It reminds the driver that he may lose business by giving snarly service, or by looking like a vagabond. He may practice on his customers some of the rudiments of courtesy.

The importance of customer communication in car retailing is emphasized by Pia Flury, a Swiss automobile salesperson [97]:

> For me a very important point is the communication between a customer and salesman, because this can develop a relationship of trust. Such trust can give the customer the confidence that he can sign a purchase contract without having mixed feelings about the decision. Only if we are able to win the trust of customers will we be regarded by them as competent professionals.

'PERSONABLE RATHER THAN PERSONAL, ALWAYS COURTEOUS, NEVER INSENSITIVE'

The experience of First Direct, a British telephone banking organization, suggests that it is not always essential for the customer to be dealt with by the same person. What is more important is that the person be pleasant and capable and also have access to the record of the customer – as all of First Direct's telephone operators do.

Said a First Direct customer, 'I've been with First Direct for two and a half years and I'm still waiting to talk to someone who isn't one of the most pleasant, friendly persons in the world. Whatever time of day or night I call, it's a pleasure to talk to them.'

With this customer-responsive performance First Direct does away with the barriers imposed by old-fashioned banking, characterized by its head, Kevin Newman, as 'the relationship of parent to child'.

Newman's objective has been to develop a service 'as I would like to be treated myself, in a way that is personable rather than personal, always courteous, never insensitive'. Rather than child to parent, the relationship is intended to be adult to adult. A better definition of good customer relations would be hard to find.

FOR THE PEOPLE-TO-PEOPLE TOUCH
GOOD TRAINING IS ESSENTIAL

The advocates of customer-pleasing personal contact emphasize that it doesn't happen by chance. Both careful selection and intensive training must play a part. 'Ability to please the customer should be, for good management, top priority for hiring and training of employees,' advised Deming.

'My impression is that many people that serve customers in restaurants, hotels, elevators, banks and hospitals would enjoy the job much more were it not that customers come in and interrupt their conversations,' said Deming, who gave a telling example [14]:

> The woman that runs the elevator in the department store plays an important role in the customer's opinion of the quality of everything for sale in the store. The Japanese know this. The woman that runs the elevator in the department store in Japan receives training over a period of two months on how to direct people, on how to answer questions, and how to handle them in a crowded elevator – this in spite of the gracious manners in a Japanese home.

Well-trained personal contact in the place of business is the touchstone of customer satisfaction, according to Anita Roddick of Britain's Body Shop chain [96]:

> We have found that when you take care of customers extremely well, and make them the focal point, never once forgetting that your first line of customers is your own staff, profitability flows from that. We achieve that by: suggestion boxes in every store, staff training, and opening the training school to customers.

Does the Body Shop method work? The chain has enjoyed remarkable profitability. Most importantly, in the context of this chapter, it does not use paid advertising. The Body Shop relies on creative public relations and the most powerful communications medium of all: word-of-mouth recommendations by satisfied customers.

CAREFUL SELECTION
AS IMPORTANT AS THOROUGH TRAINING

Tom Farmer of the Kwik-Fit chain is a firm advocate of going beyond satisfied customers to delighted customers. He explains:

> Satisfied customers have only been given what they expected. That's no longer enough. You have to go the extra mile and give something that isn't expected. Today, everybody is selling quality goods at the same price, so you have to find other ways of being different – of adding value for the customer.
>
> That invariably comes down to inter-personal relationships, how the person serving you relates to you. So we've sharpened up our recruitment so that the people we employ are right for Kwik-Fit – and Kwik-Fit is right for them.

This marked a change in recruitment by Kwik-Fit, which previously had suffered severely from heavy staff turnover in the first six months of employment. More rigorous recruitment and induction dramatically reduced the turnover rate.

BETTER CANDIDATES FROM
MORE-ADVANCED SELECTION METHODS

Aspen Tree Software of Laramie, Wyoming has developed specialized software that can be used to allow a person being recruited to communicate anonymously with a computer before a formal interview is conducted. The computer asks such sensitive questions as why the person left their last job, how they would rate their own performance, how often they get frustrated, how well they get along with their supervisors and how they rate their own organizational skills, as well as a number of other questions which can be answered according to a multiple-choice system.

From the responses the computer program generates a list of the key questions that the human interviewer should ask the applicant. It also takes note of any question which the applicant took an unusually long amount of time to answer – on the basis that their delay may flag a less-than-truthful answer.

Another method of assessing job applicants is to employ an outside survey company to carry out an initial interview. The well-known polling organization Gallup carries out this service for US companies, helping identify the life themes of prospective employees. Through a carefully-structured telephone interview, Gallup can help determine whether an employee has the attributes that fit the job at hand.

These measures do not mean that the recruitment advisor abdicates responsibility for candidate selection. One recruiter checks the way that candidates walk to the office from their car for an interview, to see whether they are purposeful or languid. Then after the interview she walks them back to their car so that she can see how clean it is – or isn't.

RECRUITMENT AIM: EMPOWERED EMPLOYEES

The ultimate aim of more informed recruiting is to achieve the best possible match between the company's aims and philosophy and its employees, so that people will be happy in their work. Says Jack Welch of General Electric, 'You can't have satisfied customers unless you have satisfied employees to serve them.'

Ed Hagenlocker of Ford develops the same theme: ' "Empowered People" is one of our underlying strategies for our vision of the future. It is our goal to make Ford the *employer of choice* ... to have Ford employees, as we say in marketing terms, completely or very satisfied.' 'Empowerment' to Ford means that its employees are trained, authorized, motivated and encouraged to contribute to their company's activities and welfare. Could Ford move beyond that to 'delighted' employees? Is this a contradiction in terms? In our view, most assuredly not.

THINK OF YOUR AUDIENCES AS YOUR 'CHEERING SECTION'

Companies of all kinds often take far too narrow a view of their audiences. By doing so they lose the opportunity to assemble a larger, more diversified congregation of enthusiastic supporters. Among such 'unexpected supporters' are those whose warm approval of a customer's purchase can do more than anything else to make them feel good about their decision.

We call this larger group of people the 'cheering section'. They are not directly involved, but they have an opinion. People have long-term associations with sports teams, religions, political affiliations and other commitments outside their work and families. To what extent does the same apply to their interest in automobiles? How can car manufacturers develop and profit from their own 'cheering sections'?

David Heslop, Managing Director of Mazda Cars UK, points out that the world's oldest, largest and wealthiest organization, the Roman Catholic Church, enjoys the support of [98] 'a dedicated group of people from outside the direct employ of the organisation itself'. They extend its reach and influence far beyond the capabilities of the 'professional' Church. In this case, is the cheering section also the customer body?

NOTHING BEATS A PERSONAL RECOMMENDATION
OF A CAR OR DEALER

The cheering section analogy reminds us not to overlook all the people outside the auto companies and their dealers who could be described as making up 'a dedicated group' who particularly favour or support specific automotive brands. They are members of car marque clubs, motor-sports enthusiasts, readers of car magazines and non-franchised repair specialists, just to name the hard-core members.

The members of the cheering section are very influential. Their views can be negative as well as positive. Their support can and must be earned over long periods. At one and the same time they are audiences and communicators. No car company, no matter how large, can afford to overlook their role or take their allegiance for granted.

For dealers a cheering section is just as important. Carl Sewell calls it 'the rock-in-the-pool theory'. 'When we do a real good job for customers,' said Sewell [63], 'they tell their friends. That word-of-mouth advertising is stronger than anything we can do on television. In fact our advertising line is, "Ask the person who drives one".'

GOOD CAUSES CAN PROVIDE
ADDED CHEERING SECTIONS

Like all large organizations, car producers and their dealers are under pressure from various directions to be more responsive to the needs of good causes. Any company that intends to be considered a good citizen in its city, state, country or even on this planet must be responsive to the needs of causes.

Evidence is not conclusive that such support translates itself into customer interests. In a 1993 survey in the USA, 66% of respondents said that they were likely to switch brands if by doing so they were supporting a cause that was of particular concern to them. On the other hand, 58% of the respondents believed that such cause-related marketing was 'just for show'. Only one in eight said that they considered assistance to a good cause to be one of the most important factors in a purchase decision.

Against these findings must be set the value of having the endorsement, even if only implied, of the members of a charitable or not-for-profit organization. That is not easily obtained. Depending on the product or service, it may well be worthy of a level of financial or other support. Vauxhall certainly thought so when its Director of Public Affairs was made a board member of the NSPCC, a leading British charity, in front of an auditorium full of its leading committee members, in recognition of his and Vauxhall's support of the charity.

DEALERS NEED CHEERING SECTIONS TOO

Dealers need to build strong direct relationships with their customers. An important tool for dealers could and should be conferences held from time to time with customers. For dealers, however, the organization of such meetings is not as commonplace as it is for the research organizations retained by the car producers. Thus some guidelines for their conduct are important.

For such conferences dealers need to engage a neutral moderator. He or she represents neither the dealer nor the customers but rather seeks to draw out views without stifling debate or adding his or her own personal opinions. Such people as journalists, sales trainers, market researchers and businesspeople, particularly from other branches, can be useful as moderators.

In addition the dealer organizing the conference may have some key questions in mind for which they are seeking answers. These should be organized in advance so that the moderator has them readily to hand. The questions should be closely related to particular problems that the dealer perceives in their relationships with customers.

The attendees for each conference should be selected according to the particular themes that are under discussion. If issues relate to the workshop, for example, the invitees should be those who have had their cars repaired at the dealership in the last two or three months. If the emphasis is on the sales side, then new-car buyers would be invited.

As a rule of thumb, in large cities invitations should be extended about two weeks before the date of the conference. To facilitate attendance, the conference should begin around six to seven o'clock in the evening and last no more than one and a half hours.

Although such meetings can be held at the dealership, it can be advantageous to organize them at hotels or restaurants with meeting-room facilities. This also enhances a 'neutral' impression. Moreover it assists in arranging for a buffet supper after the conference to thank the attendees.

TRANSCRIBED CONFERENCE FINDINGS PRESERVE CONFIDENTIALITY

Such a conference should be tape-recorded and the participants must be advised of this in advance. The recording is not the final product, however. Instead it should be transcribed to a text which is more neutral, devoid of specific identification of the participants and preventing the attendees from being recognized by their voices.

Then the results should be reviewed by the dealer principal and their key personnel. Experience has shown that this can have a devastating impact, because these people are seldom happy to be criticized.

In interpreting such findings it must be borne in mind that whatever customers perceive is valid as a perception, whether or not the basis for their perception is technically valid.

Finally, a key element of such conferences is that conclusions must be drawn and acted upon from their findings. As well, dealership management must follow up to ensure that the recommended steps to meet customer requirements are in fact being implemented.

BRANDS MUST EXPRESS
A COVENANT WITH THE CUSTOMER

According to Laurel Cutler [94], 'The "masses" have now become "individuals" – highly selective individuals – and this is one of the great forces that will drive consumer buying habits. In the 1990s, consumers will build an arching structure of behaviour which will bypass the boring middle.'

Cutler asks, 'What do we have to do to win that consumer over? I believe a large part of the answer lies in building, focusing and protecting strong brands. In the '90s, I hope that we'll all learn that a successful brand can't be all things to all people. It must make a statement to, and for, the user. It must be distinctive, unique. A brand must be focused to a consumer segment, not against some competitor.'

Laurel Cutler describes a brand as 'a covenant between a company and a customer', a promise that earns respect by being kept: 'The trick for all of us, as we move forth into the 1990s, will be to determine exactly which promises the consumer wants us to keep, and then to make absolutely certain that we do in fact keep them, avoiding the all-too-tempting compromises along the way.'

VOLVO'S RESOLUTE COMMITMENT
TO ITS BRAND PROMISE

Volvo exemplifies a brand that has kept its promises to customers for years. 'Advertising copywriter David Abbott identified the virtues of reliability, safety, longevity and quality for Volvo,' writes Stephen Bayley [99].

> Their advertising is a long-term campaign, building on Volvo's virtues rather than denying its vices of dullness and ugliness.
>
> Abbott thinks that the Volvo has never been a pretty car, so Volvo buyers believe they are making a rational choice, a decision between heart and mind. In the USA they even ran a tag line on Volvo: 'The car for people who think.' It is, as David Abbott puts it, the prestige of intellect rather than the prestige of money.

One reason why the Volvo commitment has been so unwavering is that the concept originates with the company, not with its advertising

Fig. 8.2 Volvo builds cars that look so convincingly practical and functional – 'unpretty' – that a Volvo driver must be seen as having selected a 960 for its qualities, not its looks.

agency. Over the years Volvo has provided its sales operations throughout the world with strict requirements for the key brand elements that all communications must emphasize. Latitude is given to the local staff and agency to find the best way to deliver that message in the national or regional idiom and style. But the message must remain the same everywhere.

POST-DECISION REINFORCEMENT OF PURCHASE IS VALUABLE

Stephen Bayley adds [99], 'The important principle is that most car advertising is aimed at people who have already bought the car! According to Abbott: "Advertising reassures them in their choice and they become evangelists for the marque. The product is the hero of the advertising." '

They will become evangelists, that is, if their expectations have not been raised too high. 'In the Taurus's case,' said Bill Fleming of J. D. Power [6], 'Ford did a great job in promoting their car. They really played up the "Quality is Job 1" in the ads.' Luckily, the Taurus had enough in its favour to convince early buyers that its initial quality problems weren't too serious.

'Fleming adds that auto makers can heighten the expectations of new car owners too much,' wrote Lindsay Brooke. 'He says that all manufacturers run a risk of letting their marketing and advertising get out ahead of a vehicle's actual initial quality performance in the marketplace.' In fact durability paragon Volvo successfully survived just such a disparity between its advertised reputation and a spate of serious quality problems in the 1970s.

PUBLISHING YOUR PROMISES MEANS YOU HAVE TO KEEP THEM

'Companies win business by promising service and retain business by keeping this promise.' So says David Freemantle. If the promise is published, as part of a brand statement or claim, it is a powerful incentive for all in the organization to make good on it.

'Keeping the service promise is such a basic test that it is both surprising and frustrating that so many organizations fail to pass it,' writes Freemantle [76]. 'Keeping the service promise should be an absolute priority for any manager intent on achieving success on the customer service front. Your own personal credibility is at stake when you make promises and fail to delivery on them. The more promises you and your team make, the more you keep and the better the service!'

Communications can and must be used to inform the customer if there's any danger that the service promise won't be kept, says Freemantle:

> Whatever happens, if the service promise to the customer cannot be kept, it is imperative that you inform them before they inform you. You create goodwill by contacting customers about problems before they find out about them some other way. By the time a customer starts chasing you, he or she feels bad and will have been alienated to a degree.
>
> In these days of the car phone, mobile phones, phone cards, fax machines and couriers, there is absolutely no excuse for a failure to communicate when things go wrong. Even when things are going right goodwill be gained when your staff take the initiative to communicate with the customer, to inform him or her that everything is in hand, that progress is being made, that things will happen when they say it will happen.

MAKING YOUR COMMITMENT PUBLIC IS A POWERFUL MOTIVATOR

In June 1993 Ford's Parts and Service Division changed its name to reflect its new mission. The new name is 'Ford Customer Service Division'. The Division said at the time that the change was made 'to reflect our vision and our goal . . . to provide customers with an ownership experience that is so good they will buy again, and tell others how great it is to own a Ford product.'

Stating a goal clearly and openly communicates a leadership challenge to people inside the organization in addition to informing those outside. That was a lesson that then-Lieutenant H. Norman Schwartzkopf learned when he was assigned to a reconnaissance or 'recon' platoon in West Berlin where, he wrote [100], 'units understood their mission, trained hard, and were ready for battle'. He added:

> Our troops were handpicked by the battle group personnel officer, and the belief that we were the very best permeated everything we did. We even had a sign on the door of our weapons storage room that read:

> **RECON WEAPONS**

> Best Weapons Room in the Battle Group

> The men knew that every inspector who saw that would vow, 'I'll show these guys.' But we *knew* our weapons maintenance was that good. By setting a standard of excellence in keeping to it, we built our pride and morale even higher.

INTERNAL COMMUNICATIONS SUPPORTS CONTACT WITH CUSTOMERS

With their sign, the soldiers were setting a target for themselves as well as informing others of their excellence. They were using the power of internal communication to help maintain high standards.

Company communications, of course, can be a haphazard affair. Bill Quirke, a consultant with London's Synopsis Communication, holds that these aspects of internal communication are common to most organizations:

- Most people prefer to hear things through their immediate boss.
- People are most interested in information about their own immediate work unit.
- Managers want more information but, at the same time, they complain about being swamped with paper.
- The grapevine is the most-used, though least-preferred, way of finding out about things.

IMPROVING THE QUALITY AND SPIRIT OF MANUFACTURER/DEALER COMMUNICATIONS

Within a car company's field network, communications with dealers need just as much care and attention as those with personnel. Valuable though dealer councils have been in representing the interests of dealers and manufacturer level, some manufacturers are moving to new ways of working with dealers and their representatives.

In 1993, for example, Volvo Cars North America Inc. established an eight-member executive committee chaired by the company's Executive Vice President. Half the members of the executive committee are dealers invited to join.

Volvo Cars feels that the more collegiate and co-operative atmosphere of the executive committee marks a big improvement over the former dealer council. It considered that the formal system of election and resolution made the old council a 'legalistic and adversarial forum'. Some dealers feel that this new means of communication is helping Volvo Cars exceed even Saturn as an organization that takes the views of its dealers into account.

ACTIVE SUPPORT AT TOP LEVELS IS ESSENTIAL FOR SUCCESS

General Motors is placing heavy emphasis on internal communications as it seeks to satisfy its customers better. GM's head of Public Affairs says [101] that his first priority is to 'communicate to our people what total customer satisfaction means for the focus of each business unit and each employee. Most of our communication is happening at the local level, where it is most meaningful to employees.

'This is a very individualized message,' the GM executive added. 'A research scientist and a foundry worker and an accountant all have to do very different things to make their customers totally satisfied. And only they can determine what that is.' But if GM can convince them that real customer satisfaction is a priority goal and give them the tools they need to achieve it, the programme will be successful.

Most importantly, the GM effort has the active support of the people at the top: 'The North American Operations [NAO] leadership team is supporting that effort. Members of the NAO Strategy Board are making time during visits to our operations to sit with small groups of employees to talk and to listen. It's more time-consuming and less dramatic than some of our past communication efforts, but we are convinced that it will also be more effective.'

LEADERSHIP COMMITMENT A KEY INGREDIENT

In summary, we have learned that good communication needs a powerful message, accurate targeting, allocation of resources, long-term consistency, first-class organization, scale economies, a direct sense of the marketplace and a personal touch.

Above all, said Professor Rosabeth Moss Kanter, it needs leadership:

The most powerful way to encourage people to embrace change is to develop a shared vision of an even more positive future, a vision created jointly by all of a corporation's shareholders, its customers, suppliers, employees and its potential industry and government partners.

In short the post-entrepreneurial organisation is created by a three-part mix: by the context set at the top, the values and goals emanating from top management; by the channels, forums, programmes and relationships designed in the middle to support these values and goals, and by the project ideas bubbling up from below – ideas for new ventures or technological innovations or better ways to serve customers – leaders have a role to play in each element!

WHAT BUSINESS ARE WE IN?
IS IT CARS OR TRANSPORTATION?

A leader in the airline industry puts the communications emphasis on the service he sells, not on the equipment. Managing Director of Virgin Atlantic, Syd Pennington, says:

> We communicate the core principle that we fly *people*, not planes. If someone has a bad flight we can't replace it – and that passenger is likely to tell seventeen people. If he has a good experience he only tells four. In promoting this culture we are absolutely open with all our staff. We run communication sessions to explain how we are developing the business and encourage staff to let us know their ideas and suggestions for improving the business.

Also very important to Virgin is the quality of person they hire to represent the company. Says Virgin Personnel Director Nick Potts, 'As a rule of thumb, 90% of your image of a person is framed within the first nine seconds of meeting them. So it's extremely important that you are welcomed with a smile by somebody who makes eye contact and shakes your hand. That frames your attitude to the service you arc going to gct.'

'We also want staff who are confident enough to approach new people all the time and calm enough to deal with the situation in front of people they have never met before,' he added. That sounds like a good enough description of the standard of customer contact we need in car retailing and servicing.

POINTS FOR DISCUSSION AND REVIEW

- Why is 'brand salience' important in the car markets of today and tomorrow? Discuss three examples.
- What comes first and why: a great product or a great marketing idea?
- Targeted marketing is needed. Brainstorm with your team as many ideas for customer-targeted marketing as you can.
- Who could be part of the 'cheering section' for your organization? List and discuss candidates.
- Why is it important to publish your promises to your customers?
- To satisfy your customers you must know the real purpose of your business. Consider and discuss what your business really does.

9 Coping with the customer-driven challenge

We do not suggest that asking the customer to rescue car businesses will be the easiest solution. We do suggest that it is the *only* solution – but it requires hard work, work that is, in many instances, unfamiliar. It is much easier to command customers to buy and to scorn them as unfit or unwise if they do not. But many examples have proven that this does not work.

In this chapter we conclude with some observations about the achievement of customer satisfaction in the real world. It is here, in the implementation process, that the hard work must be done. We also put forward our ideas about the structure of the ideal customerized retail dealership.

CALCULATING THE VALUE OF A CUSTOMER

In case we need reminding why we are interested in this subject, remarks by John Towers, Rover Group Chief Executive, are relevant:

> The objective isn't just to win a sale. It must be to create a bond. The customer who buys a new car every three years between the ages of 20 and 65, and invests £250 000, is our lifeblood. It should be the case that he'll be inclined to make the whole of that investment in one dealer and one manufacturer. All he needs is encouragement.

This illustrates the reason why we must take an interest in every individual customer. Each represents the potential for future business worth a quarter of a million pounds. But is it realistic to expect that customer to stay with one dealer and one marque of car throughout their entire driving lifetime? In one case, probably not; in the other, possibly. We discuss which is which and why.

CONCEPT OF OWNER LOYALTY
IS OUTDATED AND MISLEADING

Beloved though it is of our colleagues at all levels of the motor industry, the concept of loyalty to a car marque must be seen as obsolete. The idea of somehow chaining customers to our brand or marque is appealing – but in the buyers' market it is not a realistic expectation. Customers face too many appeals from too many directions. Their loyalty – if they have any – is tested too severely.

Car manufacturers are obsessed with the concept of customer loyalty. They believe that loyalty is highly desirable – 'One point of loyalty is $100 million in profits,' said a Ford executive – and make extensive efforts through communications and other means to increase loyalty.

Unfortunately for these efforts the evidence that they actually improve loyalty is not easily come by. In the USA, for example, surveys of loyalty between 1985 and 1992 showed it at levels roughly between 30% and 35% of purchasers of new cars who bought a make that was the same as their trade-in or the car that they sold [53]. In 1994 the loyalty rate stood only a fraction higher at 36.2%. Thus moving the needle on loyalty has proved to be difficult.

Owner loyalty to marques in the USA is weakest among people under 45 years old [61]. This is a very important buyer group, representing as it does the future of sales for the industry. It is doubly significant because the Japanese brands are cited as controlling a 50% share of the car owners in this segment.

FOCUS NEEDED
ON CUSTOMER SATISFACTION INSTEAD

Fundamentally the concept of owner loyalty is flawed. It is flawed because it implies that a certain body of customers exists whose fealty to the marque can be taken for granted. We have read earlier how much less it costs to sell a car to an existing owner than to conquer a new one. This comparison serves only to arouse unrealistic expectations in the minds and hearts of industry executives, especially those in the finance departments.

The product is our primary means of keeping existing owners and users loyal to our marque. If it is working well and giving pleasure we are winning the battle. But not even the perfect product will bring all its owners back to the brand. Drivers of the Lexus LS400 report virtually unanimous satisfaction with their cars. Yet almost one in five will consider another marque next time. As we saw earlier they just want a change, 'a different style'.

Today and tomorrow no customer can be taken for granted. Rather, the emphasis should and must be on treating *every* customer, including current owners, as well as possible. Because we have direct access to our current customers we must exploit that access; to ignore them would be even worse. But as a mind-set we must embrace all past, present and potential customers with equal fervour. No other approach will be good enough.

Customer satisfaction, too, is a moving target. With all manufacturers and dealers improving their performance, the rate of overall car-ownership satisfaction will improve. However, differentials between marques are likely to remain. Also, new marques will enter the arena, some inevitably at lower levels to start with. Clearly the advantage will go to those organizations that are able to make customer-satisfying improvements most rapidly and thoroughly.

CAR INDUSTRY CRAVES 'MAGIC BULLET' SOLUTIONS

The idea that complete loyalty would be the answer to all our problems, if we could only achieve it, is a typical car industry ambition. The auto industry loves the 'magic bullet' approach to problem-solving. It never loses hope that it will discover one big bold single solution to all its problems, including those of customer retention, customer relations and customer satisfaction.

As a corollary to this the auto companies, especially in the USA, seem to be able to deal with only one big problem at a time. They have difficulty in coping effectively with a wide range of challenges simultaneously. This is symptomatic of the 'magic bullet' or 'big bang' theory of corporate action. Companies hope to make the 'big play' by concentrating their corporate efforts on one spectacular objective. In this alone they will not find success.

Although this can be amply documented, one example will suffice. In the era of Roger Smith's stewardship of General Motors, the company concentrated heavily on increased manufacturing automation while neglecting car styling and design. Unfortunately the automation did not bring the needed productivity benefits and GM soon found itself lagging behind its rivals in product design.

For BMW the acquisition of Rover was a 'big bang'. But underlying and supporting the success of this initiative was the hard work at every level that everyone in BMW has been putting into the essentials of the company's business for decades. It was a reward for hard work, not a substitute for it.

COPING WITH FAILURE
IS HARD FOR THE CAR INDUSTRY

A major flaw of the 'big bang' approach is that it carries the potential for big failure as well as big success. And failure in the car industry – or what is perceived as failure – carries a lethal stigma. Executives who have 'failed' seldom maintain power in the same company and may even be driven out of the industry.

Failure, however, is overwhelmingly and increasingly inevitable. In 1993 a Chicago consulting firm, Kuczmarski & Associates, studied the successes achieved by 11 000 new products launched by 77 companies in a variety of industries. Five years after launch, they discovered, only 56% of these were still on the market. Of total investments in new-product development, almost half (46%) is spent on failures, found consultants Booz Allen & Hamilton [102].

Will shrewder planning, researching and decision making reduce the ratio of flops to successes? The prospects are not promising. A British government study [7] concluded that the outlook is for 'more uncertainty, stemming from a wider range of customers, shorter product life cycles and more competition. This means *greater uncertainty* [emphasis added] about the life of products and investment decisions associated with them.'

Though we may get smarter, the market's whimsical, fickle vagaries will outpace our ability to forecast its needs. Difficult though this conclusion is to accept in the car industry, *we must accept it*. More and more car makers are putting products into more and more segments and niches. Not all of them can or will be successful. Thus we must adjust to the inevitability of failure and develop it into a learning experience.

CUSTOMER SATISFACTION IS A MOVING TARGET

Only the customerized organization will be responsive to the fast and unpredictable changes in markets and in customer desires. The master of measuring automotive customer satisfaction, J. David Power, stressed in a talk that customerization should become an ingrained part of a company's philosophy, not an end in itself [1]:

> The rewards for providing satisfying experiences for customers will go to those manufacturers, distributors and retailers who recognise that consumers have not been in expectation hibernation while they have been absent from dealerships. These shoppers will have, in all probability, considered their next car purchase for quite some time, and when they return to the showrooms they will be bringing with them their current expectations, which are continually increasing, for what will constitute excellence in owner satisfaction. These expectations are going to figure prominently in not only their decision criteria on what car to buy but in their satisfaction with the retailer they buy their car from as well.

Dave Power thus emphasized that customer satisfaction is a moving target. Only the organization that makes it an integral part of its operations will keep advancing its standards to meet the new expectations of the customer.

'The many choices the customer has today plus all the information the customers now receive make a very dynamic environment,' Power added. 'So expectations are constantly rising.' Those expectations must be met – and quickly – at every point of contact with the customer.

FAILURE MUST BE EXPLOITED AS A LEARNING EXPERIENCE

We conclude that product, system and service failure is so unavoidable that it should be an understood part of corporate life. However, failure can and does carry value to those capable of learning.

Its appreciation of the inevitability of failure has contributed much of the strength of the Japanese motor industry. Less personalized and politicized than their Western counterparts, the Japanese car makers concentrate on understanding failures and drawing lessons from them. Their executives and engineers are highly motivated to try to do better next time. They bounce back and try again.

Meanwhile, their contemporaries in the West are preoccupied with the allocation of blame and the smearing of reputations in the highly political environments of their companies. Western car companies have cloudy rear-view mirrors. They are poor at looking back and learning from failures.

Fig. 9.1 A clearer 'rear-view mirror' might have helped GM realize that the two-seater configuration of its prototype Impact electric car necessarily limited its market appeal.

GM'S RELUCTANCE TO LEARN FROM EXPERIENCE

General Motors has a rich lode of failures to mine for its edification. The Pontiac Fiero, skyrocketing to sensational sales and then collapsing. The Buick Regatta, a two-seater personal car with an abbreviated life span. The Cadillac Allanté, dropped after seven model years. The short-lived Elan, produced by its Lotus subsidiary.

Yet GM seems unwilling or unable to conduct post-mortems on these casualties in order to learn from the losses they sustained. In 1993 GM postponed plans to produce its Impact electric car. Market surveys had shown that its two-seater design lacked sufficient appeal. The cars in the previous paragraph that had so disappointed GM were all two-seaters. A clearer rear-view mirror would have helped. Perhaps as the 'EV-1' the car will fare better.

Cadillac's Allanté emerged from the womb handicapped. To be sure it had quality problems at launch, but those could be dealt with. Cadillac recommended keeping the Allanté's price below the critical $50 000 barrier. It would already be the most costly Cadillac by far; the GM division wanted to launch at a lower price, establish the product and exploit it later. Market research showed a good chance of conquering the aged Mercedes-Benz SL with this strategy. But the command came down from the corporation to price higher: $54 700 at launch. The Allanté never recovered.

Fig. 9.2 Instead of being launched at less than $50 000, a barrier no Cadillac had ever crossed, the Allanté was burdened by an initial price of $54 700. It never really recovered.

FOCUS ON FAILURE LIMITS OPTIONS

Companies obsessed by their failures experience a dangerous narrowing of the options available to them. For a generation of managers after the controversial Airflow of the 1930s, the poor acceptance of that car was taken as a sign not only to its maker, Chrysler, but also to the whole American industry that innovating too fast was too risky.

Germany's Porsche is a case in point. Still owned by its founding family, it carries a huge burden of tradition – not all of it successful. Its low-cost sports car built at an Audi plant, the 924/944, is seen as a failure. So that option is closed. Recent ventures in racing at Indy and in Formula 1 were flops. So those options are closed. Porsche is an example of a company so tightly corseted by what it perceives as its failures that it finds any new movement difficult.

Concluded management analysts Hammer and Champy [13], 'Management systems should reward people who try good ideas that fail, not punish them. At Motorola the motto is, "We *celebrate* noble failure." An organization that demands constant perfection discourages people from striving and makes them timid.' We would only take issue with their reference to 'good ideas'. An idea that failed is never later considered to be a 'good idea'. But failure, even with a promising idea, should not be condemned.

CAR INDUSTRY EXCESSIVELY INTOLERANT
OF RISK-TAKERS

People daring unorthodox solutions are apt to be denied acceptance in most car companies. Would-be corporate innovators receive this warning from Hal Sperlich [12]: 'You're walking a very lonely road. Life in a large corporation is easier if you go with the flow and don't support major change. People who propose things that are different make more conservative people nervous, and the corporate environment just doesn't reward people for challenging the status quo.'

Before its launch the Ford Taurus, Ford's most successful car of recent years, was judged likely to be a flop in the market by many of Ford's senior executives. To a colleague who had contributed to the Taurus's conception a top Ford man shouted, 'This car will ruin the Ford Motor Company *and it will be your fault!*' That the Taurus was a success only intensified the senior executive's anger. The colleague? He left Ford.

Companies trying to make major changes encounter two main obstacles among their personnel: fear and the desire to protect turf. Managers fear that their many years of experience in existing jobs will no longer be of value in a new organization with new ideas.

Even though the objective of much business restructuring is to reduce the influence of senior managers, such managers nevertheless must support any major changes. Ford's Climate Control Division wanted to reduce dramatically the time it took to develop new heating and air-conditioning systems. The Division's designers and engineers strongly resisted the proposed changes. Only after the support of senior managers was vouchsafed was it possible to introduce new time-saving methods.

Customer needs can only be met if all levels of a company welcome new ideas, are willing to take risks and acknowledge the inevitability of failure. By monitoring risk, the impact of failure can be manageable. And step after novel step the company and its products will come closer to meeting the needs of its present and future customers.

ACHIEVE SUCCESS THROUGH MANY SMALL YET STEADY IMPROVEMENTS

The achievement of customer satisfaction is not easy. There is no single, simple answer. Instead participants in the industry, from designer through production engineer to marketer and distributor, must consider the customer at every stage of the car's life from its initial conception to its final scrapping.

Donald E. Petersen provides an example of the approach needed, based on his experience with Ford [17]:

> For too many decades Ford, as well as thousands of other US companies, had a superficial and single-dimensional definition of quality that almost entirely concerned objective measurements, or the number of things that went wrong. Our biggest mistake was not being driven by what customers wanted and not making a disciplined effort to examine the subjective side – the intangible look and feel that attracts customers to particular cars. The most important thing we learned this past decade is that all those elements that appeal to a customer, that are intangibly right, must be considered a part of the overall quality of the product.

Through his contacts with Mazda, of which Ford is a part owner, Don Petersen discovered that a more profound, less superficial approach to product improvement could be more satisfying to the customer: 'In the mid-1980s Mr. Yamamoto of Mazda described to me the concept the Japanese call *kansei*, which is the oneness of the product with the user. *Kansei* takes into account all the intangible things that make the customer feel both confident and right at home when he or she steps into a well-designed car.'

BECOME A 'CUSTOMER-CREATING AND CUSTOMER-SATISFYING' COMPANY

Doing all the small things well (consistent with *kansei*) is the key to the achievement of customer satisfaction. 'The entire corporation must be viewed as a customer-creating and customer-satisfying organism,' wrote Harvard's Theodore Levitt in his pioneering article, *Marketing Myopia* [103]. 'Management must think of itself not as producing products but as providing customer-creating satisfactions. It must push this idea (and everything it means and requires) into every nook and cranny of the organisation.'

Doing this is not easy, Levitt warned. There is no 'magic bullet' for customer satisfaction: 'Building an effective customer-oriented company involves far more than good intentions and promotional tricks; it involves profound matters of human organisation and leadership.' It requires application of the 'noodle factor' to all aspects of a company's business.

A common saying in commerce and industry is 'if it ain't broke, don't fix it'. Customerizing goes well beyond this. 'If it isn't broken, break it', recommend Diners Club and British Airways in their report, *Negotiating the Nineties*. They urge companies to 'go looking for problems'. This is another way of saying that they can achieve customer satisfaction only through corporate dissatisfaction.

BECOME A 'REORGANIZATION-PROOF' COMPANY

In 210 BC Petronius Arbiter wrote, 'We trained hard ... but it seemed that every time we were beginning to form up into teams we would be reorganised. I was to learn later in life that we tend to meet any new situation by reorganising; and a wonderful method it can be for creating the illusion of progress while producing confusion, inefficiency and demoralisation.'

This quotation has become part of the underground communication flow in companies that have suffered from 'reorganize-itis'. General Motors is the most conspicuous example in the motor industry; its creation of an unwieldy group structure in the 1980s served only to make it more remote from its customers, not closer to them.

The traditional Western company structure, operating on a top-down basis, is particularly well suited to constant reorganization. Viewing the company from the top its executives find it easy and interesting to redraw organization charts linking corporate boxes in one new way or another. This is an effective manner of seeming to generate change; as Petronius Arbiter said, the main consequence is confusion.

'THANK GOD FOR THE FROZEN MIDDLE'

Middle managers in most companies know this. When new structures are imposed from the top down they drag their feet. 'How long will this last?' they ask. 'Whose idea is this? Oh, he won't be around very long.' Lacking confidence in either the value or the duration of the new idea, they resist it.

This resistance is often prudent. Top managers complain about the 'frozen middle' or the 'mushy middle' in their organizations that is reluctant to make the changes they want them to make. Frankly, some car companies may owe their survival to the good sense of those managers in the middle layers who were reluctant to go along with the latest whims of their CEOs.

This point is emphasized by corporation reengineers Hammer and Champy [13]: 'Some people think companies could cure what ails them by changing their corporate strategies. They should sell one division and buy another, change their markets, get into a different business. Playing tycoon might be more exciting for senior managers than dirtying their hands in the mundane details of operations, but it is not more important.'

SATISFYING THE CUSTOMER INTERDICTS EXECUTIVE WHIMS

Tinkering with companies from the top down has strong appeal. It suits the 'magic bullet' or 'big bang' approach that car makers like. It is glamorous and creates an illusion of progress. But Hammer and Champy have found it wanting [13]:

> None of the management fads of the last twenty years – not management by objectives, diversification, Theory Z, zero-based budgeting, value chain analysis, decentralization, quality circles, 'excellence', restructuring, portfolio management, management by walking around, matrix management, intrapreneuring or one-minute managing – has reversed the deterioration of America's corporate competitive performance. They have only distracted managers from the real tasks at hand.

The authentically and thoroughly customerized company fights such fads – and 'reengineering' as well. It is virtually tinker-proof. Because it works from the bottom up, responding to changes in the market-place and to its direct knowledge of customer needs and desires, its value-adding elements are of manageable size with self-defining missions and methods.

It is much more difficult to cause chaos in such customerized companies by reorganizations. Focused on meeting the needs of the customer, their people at all levels (and there may be fewer levels) are much less easily distracted by new structures imposed from the top – to the ultimate advantage of the shareholders!

ENLIGHTENED LEADERS MUST RELINQUISH POWER TO THEIR CUSTOMERS

Though more than 30 years have passed since Theodore Levitt's pioneering article appeared, many companies have still not grasped the central role that the customer must and does play in every aspect of their business. *In Search Of Excellence* by Tom Peters and Bob Waterman states that 'despite all the lip service given to market orientation these days ... the customer is either ignored or considered a bloody nuisance'.

In the car industry there are growing exceptions, inspired by enlightened leaders. We described the importance of strong team leaders in the R&D and design phases of product creation. Leadership, of course, is needed at overall company level as well if customer satisfaction is to be accepted as a goal throughout an organization.

'There's always a guy who causes the turnaround of a major corporation,' said successful auto dealer Carl Sewell [71]. 'He can't do it by himself; it takes a team. But an enabler at the top provides the vision and direction for success. Leaders give you profitability, product; they allow a person's talent to come out and they put the best players on the field. People create the process – the process does not create the people.'

Sewell gave his view of automotive leaders in the USA:

> Chrysler's turnaround was led by Iacocca and Lutz; Ford's by Caldwell and Petersen, Trotman and Poling. GM's failures are the result of the leadership of Roger Smith. GM's turnaround will be led by Jack Smith, Bill Hoglund and J.T. Battenberg. They will determine GM's success or failure, what products are built. Alfred P. Sloan made GM a success; it will be Jack Smith who determines success from here on.

Among the Japanese makers Soichiro Honda was obsessed by technology but also had an innate sense of what would appeal to the customer. In Europe Rover has made an about-face from being one of the most autocratic companies to being customer-focused. Helmut Werner has signalled to the world that Mercedes-Benz will listen more closely to the customer from now on.

DEALER SELF-INTEREST CAN LEAD TO OPTIMUM CUSTOMER SERVICE

The factors discussed thus far have some relevance to car-dealer activities but speak more directly to the operations of the auto makers. How, more specifically, should we view the role of the dealers? They are at the point of daily contact with present and potential customers. How, and more especially why, are they to respond to the customerizing imperative?

The aim in a dealership, as in any business, must be to reduce unproductive staff and activity and instead to emphasize value-adding personnel and actions. Dealerships should be so structured and so motivated that it is obviously valuable for them to operate efficiently in order to gain the maximum amount of profit from their main mission: selling and servicing new and used cars.

We believe that this will require radical changes in the ways dealers operate. We reject the idea that dealers should be paid by car makers to take better care of their customers. The fundamental concept of dealer operations must be reviewed to illustrate and demonstrate how real customer satisfaction, achieved by doing all jobs right the first time, can and does contribute to more efficient, hence less costly, dealer operations.

Only if dealers are motivated to satisfy their customers because it is in their own self-interest, through the design of the business, will they fully embrace and implement the customerizing concept.

LOYALTY TO THE DEALER COULD BE IMPORTANT

Earlier we rejected the idea of customer loyalty to a car brand or marque. We said that it could lead to complacency about the attitudes of a critically-important customer body. But how about loyalty to car dealers? Is this equally irrelevant?

In a specific survey conducted in the USA in 1991, the loyalty level to car marques was 30% [61]. Fractionally but significantly higher than marque loyalty in 1991 was the 33% loyalty level of owners to an individual dealership. This was substantially higher than the 20% dealer loyalty figure of three years earlier [61]. Here, the record shows, progress is being made. Against all odds, customer loyalty to dealerships is increasing.

Auto makers selling in America are judged to be ambivalent at best about the possible benefits to them of higher dealer, as opposed to marque, loyalty. Yet the needs and desires of the customer must surely be met best by the stimulation of strong loyalty at the individual dealer level. Too few car makers are willing to acknowledge this. They are slow to tolerate, let alone encourage, actions to this end by dealers.

DEALER-LEVEL CUSTOMERIZATION BUILDS LOYALTY

An example of customerization in action is California's Longo Toyota dealership. Longo reckons to have a far higher rate of sales through referrals and repeat purchases than the average dealer, thanks to its customer-satisfying policies. This performance translates directly into lower advertising and promotion costs and higher profits.

When J.D. Power and Associates rated Carl Sewell's Cadillac dealership, it found that the share of Sewell's new-car buyers who were 'very satisfied' with their new Cadillac was 25% higher than the national average. The cars were the same; why was this so? Clearly Sewell's superior customer treatment made the difference.

The same survey found that the share of Sewell's customers who 'definitely would' buy a Cadillac again was 47%, against 35% nationwide [63]. The odds are that they will buy again from Sewell Village

Cadillac. This finding is reinforced by the others in this volume that report the positive influence of good servicing on repeat purchasing.

Could a dealer be so customerized that they could rely completely on repeat and word-of-mouth business? That they could do away with paid advertising altogether? Britain's Body Shop skin-care chain does just that.

MOVING BEYOND 'SATISFACTION' TO 'DELIGHT'

Especially in North America motor companies and their advisors are beginning to speak of 'delighting' customers. This is expressed as a step beyond mere 'satisfaction'. It implies that customers are more than just satisfied with a company's goods and services, indeed that they are profoundly pleased, indeed ecstatic.

Such delight is bound to yield benefits in terms of return business, whether it is generated by the product or the dealer's services or, ideally, both. But what do we really mean by 'delight'? We spoke about it in Chapter 3 in terms of product features that surprised the owner and driver in a pleasing manner. (Surprises of course are not always positive!) But is this adequate as a definition of delight? How can you tell when a customer is enthusiastic about their positive experiences?

We propose the following definition:

> The delighted customer is one who feels so satisfied that they will actively proselytize to others on behalf of a product and/or service.

The 'delighted' become your cheering section. They are so happy with your brand that they will seek out others and endeavour to convince them that they should consider a similar purchase. They are, in short, the generators of that word-of-mouth recommendation that is the most powerful marketing tool known to the industry.

SEWELL'S CHECKLIST
FOR CUSTOMER-PLEASING ACTIONS

If we are to think of improving the ability of the conventional dealership to satisfy customers, the preceding chapters will have shown many examples of good practice and provided as many recommendations for positive changes. As an example of one dealer who is pleasing customers in many ways Cadillac–Lexus dealer Carl Sewell will serve as well as any.

'Over the years,' says Sewell [63], 'we've developed a 10-point mental checklist that helps us do a job right the first time. Before we change the way we do anything, we always ask these 10 questions. Before we go ahead, we must be comfortable with the answer to each one.' Here's Sewell's list:

1. What's the benefit to the customer?
2. Will the customer easily understand that benefit?
3. What impact will this idea, programme or system have on our employees?
4. How will it affect our existing systems?
5. Is anybody else doing it successfully? What can we learn from their experience?
6. What could go wrong?
7. Will it give us an advantage over our competitors?
8. How much will it cost?
9. Will it make money?
10. When should we evaluate it?

One other question could usefully be added to this checklist: How long, and in what way, can we keep it exclusively ours? When ideas are seen to work they are quickly imitated by rivals. The best ideas have an ability to be protected for some time at least. Their protection may derive from an advantage of cost, geography, patentability, personality, difficulty of execution or some combination of these.

YOU NEED TO REDUCE COSTS THROUGH SATISFACTION, NOT INCREASE COSTS

In the context of today's dealership structure Carl Sewell's list is very useful. Thinking ahead, however, to the way that dealers could and should be structured and motivated, instead of 'How much will it cost?' one of the questions should be 'How much will it save?' Authentic customerizing actions should save money overall, not add cost.

This may seem at first sight a surprising, even impossible idea. How can customers be taken care of better without costing a dealer more – indeed by costing them less? What about all those gifts, extra services, added personnel? Won't they cost more? Some may, but they must be compensated by significant cost reductions that result from better customer care. Otherwise dealers will not move to adopt them.

Let's draw an analogy with the actions that were taken to escape from the 'bad old days' of poor product quality. Years ago, and even recently in Europe, car makers thought that good quality cost more. They thought quality was achieved by having more inspectors, more costly tooling, higher-grade materials, etc. 'How much quality can we afford?' they used to ask.

BETTER DEALERSHIP EFFICIENCY
PLEASES CUSTOMERS

The Japanese turned this idea on its head. True quality, they found, makes a car less expensive, not more expensive, to produce. It is achieved by doing everything right the first time so that there is no waste in the process. With no faulty parts there are no costly rectifications at the end of the production line. With 100% quality parts, both the component suppliers and the car assembler operate at top efficiency.

Once this principle was grasped, it became possible to motivate car makers toward quality improvement. They could see that better quality reduced cost and thereby improved their competitiveness and secured their jobs. This strong motivating factor is now accepted and is helping car makers improve quality and reduce cost at the same time throughout the world.

The same process must be initiated in customer satisfaction. Dealers must become convinced, through experience and practical example, that the achievement of genuine customer satisfaction is in their own best interests because it will make their operations more efficient, less costly and thus more profitable.

COMMON-SENSE MEASURES COST LITTLE

Some examples will illustrate the concept. Carl Sewell took an important step towards increased efficiency when he defied GM's edict to hire a customer-relations manager at his Cadillac dealership. Sewell's idea was that if all his people were concerned with customer relations, as they had to be if customers were to be well served, he didn't need the cost of this extra person. GM fought him hard – until his dealership posted sky-high CSI scores that settled the argument.

Customer satisfaction does not have to generate costs, argues Knut Schüttemeyer, Global Service Co-ordinator for the Volkswagen Group [104]:

> The quantum leap in service for me is to let the customer feel that we not only fulfil but also over-fulfil his desires. This requires a fundamentally more homogeneous commitment on the part of every single employee. It does not necessarily demand high investment.
>
> When the auto is vacuumed after repairs and perhaps returned to the customer even cleaner than it was before that produces customer satisfaction. The customer didn't expect that. There are only two kinds of ashtrays: either they have ashes or sweet papers in them. When I empty the latter and put fresh sweets in, that generates customer enthusiasm.
>
> If I can make many little steps of this kind in as many areas as possible, and when the whole dealership thinks this way and

considers it more than an advertising gimmick, then it becomes clear that the achievement of customer enthusiasm does not have to be linked with high investment. The most important rule – and this is basically quite simple – is that every employee in the dealership must understand how to handle a customer as if he is a personal friend.

NET SAVINGS AVAILABLE
FROM TRUE CUSTOMER SATISFACTION

It must be more efficient to give a car a proper pre-delivery inspection (PDI) to ensure its proper functioning than it is to fix the problems that poor PDI causes later on. This holds true even if the manufacturer is paying for the repairs under warranty. Can the dealer not thus shift costs from unpredictable repairs to a regular and consistent PDI programme?

Clear explanation of the features of the car at the start of ownership by the salesperson ensures that those features of the car give maximum satisfaction to the owner. Without it, problems could arise as a result of the owner's lack of understanding of the car. The brief time required for the explanation will save costly time later on.

From the perspective of the dealer, initiatives like these that will improve customer satisfaction may seem to be counterproductive to profitability. They may be happy to have more warranty work, not less. They may want more business in their workshop for rectification of poor original repairs or for correction of problems that have arisen from improper use of the vehicle.

If any of these is so, then this is reason enough for a rethink of the fundamental operating premises of auto dealerships, for such attitudes, aims and objectives work strongly against customer satisfaction.

DEALER STRUCTURE MUST BE REENGINEERED
TO SATISFY CUSTOMERS

To use the phrase of Hammer and Champy, we call for 'the reengineering of the auto dealership'. To quote them [13], 'Reengineering a company means tossing aside old systems and starting over. It doesn't mean tinkering with what already exists or making incremental changes that leave basic structures intact. It means asking this question: "If I were re-creating this company today, given what I know and given current technology, what would it look like?" '

Many car dealerships function well. This book is rife with good examples. But we consider that the fundamental concept of the structure of a dealership may block its achievement of its full potential for customer satisfaction. Thus a total redesign is recommended.

What form should it take? The answer comes from a look at the organizational structure of a typical dealer. The car dealership may well be the smallest business organization with the most highly developed hierarchical structure. With its traditional 'chimneys' of new-car sales, used-car sales, service and parts sales it creates highly vertical structures with the potential for a multi-layered management and sharply divided responsibilities and objectives.

CHIMNEYS STAND IN WAY OF CUSTOMER SATISFACTION

This kind of organization flies in the face of the principles that we have found to be vital to satisfying customers: empowerment of people facing customers, fast decision making, a spirit of teamwork and shared values, a strong concept well communicated and ready acceptance of the need to listen and respond.

Instead, within the relatively small organization of a dealership we have specialized department heads whose instinct, writes Christopher Lorenz [105], 'is to continue furthering their own interests. Many top managers behave, not as a cohesive team, but as warring barons, each defending their own departmental or personal constituency. They are loath to become team players – and then to challenge much of what they have stood for.'

A vertical departmental structure has traditionally been regarded as needed by the specialized nature of the various tasks that have to be performed in a dealership. Must it be so? Would it be impracticable to have cross-training of personnel so that many people in the dealership are capable of carrying out a wide variety of tasks? So that they truly operate as a team?

CREATING THE 'REENGINEERED DEALERSHIP'

It could work. A salesperson could sell parts as well as cars. A technician could rotate as needed into selling cars. Personnel now considered non-technical could be trained to perform first-echelon service tasks. People traditionally seen as clerical or non-productive could be cross-trained to handle other tasks in the dealership as well.

Giving a range of dealership posts this kind of variety and interest could lead to a substantial improvement in job satisfaction. It would create a new kind of organization that would deploy its people more usefully and productively. Probably, as well, the reengineered dealership would reduce staffing requirements.

Coupled with these advantages, the much greater sense of teamwork in the dealership of the future would bring dramatic benefits to customer satisfaction. Gone would be the 'It's not my problem' attitude that hides behind so many customer-relations failures.

Keeping customers happy, indeed delighted, would clearly be everyone's responsibility, not no one's as is too often the case today.

CONSTANT IMPROVEMENT FACILITATED AND STIMULATED BY TEAMWORK

Recommended, therefore, is the reengineering of the traditional retail dealership by eliminating the traditional vertical, hierarchical organization. A senior cadre of managers would work as a problem-solving team, ensuring that their people have the support they need. They would have specialities, but these would be in addition to their broader responsibilities.

Dealer personnel with line responsibilities would be recruited, above all, for their ability to meet and work with customers in a constructive way. Specialized training in several dealership activity areas will give them the professional skills they need. Formed into cross-functional groups, they would have considerable autonomy in deciding who among them would do which jobs at what time.

One factor will be evident from the preceding chapters: only with such an organization will constant improvement (*kaizen*) be achieved. The vertical, hierarchical dealership will robustly resist any change, especially if it promises better productivity and efficiency. Only the reengineered dealership, with teamwork and customer commitment as a way of life, would encourage steady progress toward lower operating cost combined with better customer care.

SPREAD THE SATISFACTION MISSION OVER ALL DISCIPLINES

The new-style dealership will be able to implement a customer-focused approach by taking actions over a broad range of disciplines. 'If we are to survive and thrive, we must consider new management key actions and our daily agendas must see a new set of priorities,' says Mazda UK's David Heslop. He defines some of the areas that he sees as important [98]:

1. The hiring, training and developing of the best people. If we haven't got this right, our competition will. At Mazda U.K. we now spend more than four times the annual budget of only three years ago on staff – technical, management and attitude development. In its factory at Flat Rock, USA, Mazda is spending roughly $13 000 on training per employee. There is no doubt that people are our greatest asset.

2. Measurement – a chore it may be but if we can't or don't measure, then our reactions will be too slow. Customer care is as much about knowing you've got it wrong quickly and putting it right quickly as it is about getting it right first time.

3. Pace is part of our challenge and we must bring to bear as much focused and relevant technology as we can. Examples can be found today when looking at our workshop and show-room systems compared to only a few years ago.

TAKE FULL ADVANTAGE OF COMMUNICATIONS SYSTEMS

Throughout this book the use of information systems has been empha-sized. We saw systems being used to help customers define their desired car and order it, to help the salesperson explain the merits of the car, to deliver and implement the order at the factory, to establish, maintain and use lists of customers at both dealer and manu-facturer level, to understand and act on customer complaints and to speed parts and service to customers in trouble.

Clearly the integration of the systems needed to do these jobs could only be of overall benefit to both suppliers and customers. Through teamwork in the reengineered dealership such integration could be achieved, instead of having a patchwork of different departmental computers and programmes.

An information services company, Unisys, has service-marked the term 'Customerize' to express its commitment to the creation and use of such integrated customer-pleasing systems. We can only applaud this initiative. Unisys describes its Customerize concept as [106] 'applying information technology to better serve our customers' customers'. According to Unisys, Customerize is designed to:

- Help make a company more responsive to its customers and better able to attract new ones.
- Extend an organization's information systems capabilities to field locations and other points of customer contact and support.
- Make information technology serve an organization's needs by serving the needs of its customers.

Properly deployed, information technology at this level will be invis-ible to the customer. Unisys uses the example of 'a customer-focused bank – where a service representative can call up your account on a screen and instantly tell you what you need to know about recent transactions and even give you product suggestions based on your history and investment preferences. All you know is that it means no waiting for the manager, no "we'll get back to you," no frustration.'

NEED TO CREATE A SENSE OF URGENCY

There are no secrets in customerizing companies. The concept is clear and the methods are available. Especially in difficult times, those who adopt the philosophy first will leap out ahead of their rivals. Some will gain an insuperable advantage. Thus a sense of urgency in application is needed.

Not by chance do many customer-care concepts originate in Japan. As Cedric Shimo, Vice-President of Honda International Trading says [21]:

> Contrary to what some people think, the Japanese are not better businesspeople than the Americans. But they are more service-oriented because they must be to survive in fiercely-competitive Japan.
>
> Not every Japanese company excels in servicing its customers, but the ones that don't aren't likely to succeed. In any event, only the well-operated Japanese companies – the cream of the crop – come to America. These are Japan's 'first-string' companies. The fourth- and fifth-string teams stay home or go out of business altogether.

What has happened in Japan is happening in America, which has been a buyers' market for cars for some years, and is beginning to happen in Europe. This should be inspiration enough for the taking of urgent action to meet the needs of customers at all levels of your business.

PLACE THE CUSTOMER AT THE CENTRE OF EVERY ASPECT OF THE BUSINESS

'Most managers continue to see their company's essential purpose as selling whatever production happens to make, rather than designing new products and services to suit the changing preferences of the customer,' writes business journalist Christopher Lorenz [107]:

> If a company is to respond to changing consumer preferences and to competitor actions, it must constantly question its existing strategies and tactics. Its keynote must be flexibility. Yet, constant change is anathema to most corporations. Faced with a challenge of such magnitude, it is not altogether surprising that so many managements have either funked it completely, or have failed to appreciate all the pitfalls.

'Constant change is anathema to most corporations.' How true. They long for the peace and quiet of stable exchange and interest rates, not too much government interference and just enough competition to make life interesting. Above all, they don't want to be bothered by those tiresome customers. But of course those that avoid being bothered by them, won't be so for long. They won't be long in business.

POINTS FOR DISCUSSION AND REVIEW

- Discuss with your team the factors for and against 'customer loyalty' as a key objective for your organization.
- How and why should product and service failures help you improve your ability to satisfy and even delight your customers?
- Why and how does the achievement of true customer satisfaction make a business more reorganization-proof?
- Consider and list some of the ways the structure and organization of today's car dealership works against the satisfaction of customers.
- List with your team some common-sense ideas that will increase customer satisfaction at little or no cost – or will even save money!
- Leadership is needed to make rapid change happen. Consider the leaders you know and respect and the methods that they have used to respond faster to customer needs and desires.

References

1. Power, J.D, *What Is Customer Satisfaction and How Is it Measured?*, Verlag Moderne Industrie Automobil-Forum.
2. Lowry, A.T. and Hills, N.S. (1991) *Europe in the Firing Line – Coping With the Challenge of Japanese Cars and Trucks*, Euromotor Reports, London.
3. Hills, N.S. (1992) *The Ludvigsen Car Price Report and Forecast*, Euromotor Reports, London.
4. Wormald, J. (1993) Distribution; the last frontier for competitive advantage? *Automotive Marketing Review*, May, p.8.
5. *Autofahren in Deutschland '92*, Motor-Presse, Stuttgart, 1992.
6. Brooke, L. (1990) The quest for quality. *Automotive Industries*, **170**(1), 38.
7. Roberts, T. and Smalley, M. (1993) *Manufacturing into the Late 1990s*, HMSO Publications, London.
8. Bayley, S. (1991) *Taste – The Secret Meaning of Things*, Faber and Faber, London.
9. Emmerich, E. (1992) VDA press release, Frankfurt.
10. Jackson, K., Product-driven. *Automotive News Insight*, 7 March 1994, p.16i.
11. Brandtner, M., Readers report. *Business Week*, 26 September 1994, p.4.
12. Huey, J., *Fortune*, 23 September 1991.
13. Hammer, M. and Champy, J. (1993) *Reengineering the Corporation: A Manifesto for Business Revolution*, HarperBusiness, New York.
14. Deming, W.E. (1986) *Out of the Crisis*, 2nd edn, Cambridge University Press, Cambridge.
15. Maskery, M.A. and Johnson, R., Japan's Big Five atone for sins of late '80s. *Automotive News*, 17 May 1993, p.19.
16. Lorenz, C., *Financial Times*, 26 June 1992.
17. Petersen, D.E. and Hillkirk, J. (1991) *A Better Idea – Redefining the Way Americans Work*, Houghton Mifflin, Boston.
18. Nussbaum, B. Hot products. *Business Week*, 7 June 1993, p.43.
19. Womack, J.D., Jones, D.T. and Roos, D. (1990) *The Machine That Changed the World*, Rawson Associates, New York.

20. Taub, E. (1991) *Taurus: The Making of the Car that Saved Ford*, Dutton, New York.

21. Shook, R.L. (1988) *Honda – An American Success Story*, Prentice Hall, New York.

22. Kobi, G. (1993) Fixing GM. *Automotive Industries*, **173**(6), 34.

23. Calvet, J., PSA Peugeot Citroën, speech on 8 September 1993. Note that M. Calvet is still using the rightly-discredited term 'consumer'.

24. Kobe, G. (1993) Better benchmarking. *Automotive Industries*, March, p.45.

25. Smith, D.C. (1994) Managing for change. *Ward's Auto World*, August, p.33.

26. Maioli, M., City Car Seminar, Design Museum, London, 19 April 1993.

27. Frame, P., Smith remakes GM for today's world. *Automotive News*, 17 May 1993, p.23.

28. McElroy, J. (1988) Outsourcing: the double-edged sword. *Automotive Industries*, **168**(3), 46.

29. Meroth, P. (1993) Autos? Das sollen Autos sein. *Süddeutsche Zeitung Magazin*, (16), 16.

30. Personal interview with J. Nasser, 25 June 1993.

31. Inagaki, T. (1993) Developing products in post-bubble days. *Car Styling*, March, p.6.

32. Simon, H. (1993) Stein der Weisen. *Manager Magazin*, February, p.134.

33. Giacosa, D. (1979) *Forty Years of Design with Fiat*, Automobilia, Milan.

34. Taylor, A., III, How Toyota copes with hard times. *Fortune*, 25 January 1993, p.48.

35. Bedard, P. (1992) Yea team. *Car and Driver*, **38**(6), 31.

36. Pennant-Rea, R. (1993) *A World in Flux: Opportunities and Challenges*, speech, Milton Keynes, UK.

37. Sekine, K. (1993) *Manager Magazin*, February.

38. Burgess, J. and Hiatt, F., How Toyota clung to its U.S. sales, *International Herald Tribune*, 17 February 1988.

39. Rapoport, C., How Europe can create jobs. *Fortune*, 9 August 1993.

40. Bossidy, L., corporate letter to shareholders, 8 February 1994.

41. *The Times*, London, 15 May 1994.

42. Fleming, A., In Lopez program, all manufacturing is geared to customer. *Automotive News*, 1993, p.56.

43. Sloan, A.P., Jr (1941) *Adventures of a White-Collar Man*, Doubleday, Doran & Co., New York.

44. Fleming, A., Calling all cars. *Automotive News Insight*, 28 June 1993, p.12i.

45. Rayment, T., *Sunday Times*, 2 January 1994.

46. Roudebush, R.L., President, Rockwell International Corporation, speech on 4 August 1993.

47. Flannang, J.M. (1994) Want to custom-order your next car? *Tirekicking Today*, **1**(9), 2.
48. Frame, P., 'Agile' factories may turn dealers into order-takers. *Automotive News*, 1 November 1993, p.46.
49. *Daily Mail*, London, 8 May 1993.
50. Henry, J., Volvo quietly scores big in US. *Automotive News*, 27 June 1994, p.6.
51. Rechtin, M., Buyers of Japan makes unhappy with dealers. *Automotive News*, 21 June 1993, p.44.
52. Hill, F., It's hard to part an expert from his money. *Daily Telegraph*, London, 5 June 1993.
53. Ogilvy & Mather AutoTrends Panel, 1988.
54. Connelly, M., Pricing services prosper, Power survey finds. *Automotive News*, 13 September 1993, p.4.
55. Zinn, L., Retailing will never be the same. *Business Week*, 26 July 1993, p.4.
56. Ogilvy & Mather AutoTrends Panel, 1992.
57. Krebs, M., Car makers lay down law on dealer design. *Motor Trader*, London, 7 February 1993, p.14.
58. Chappell, L., Carmakers try to make buying simple. *Automotive News*, 25 January 1993, p.3.
59. Sawyers, A., Customer One delights Chrysler. *Automotive News*, 23 August 1993, p.43.
60. Bohn, J., Chrysler enters new phase of Customer One training. *Automotive News*, 10 May 1993, p.18.
61. Ogilvy & Mather AutoTrends Panel, 1991.
62. Fisher, P. (1993) The Toyota dealer from El Monte. *Motor Trader*.
63. Sewell, C. and Brown, P.B. (1990) *Customers for Life, How to Turn That One-Time Buyer into a Lifetime Customer*, Doubleday, New York.
64. McDowell, E., A motivated staff keeps the Ritz in Ritz–Carlton. *International Herald Tribune*, 1 April 1993.
65. Maskery, M.A., Toyota cost cutting kills personalised car delivery. *Automotive News*, 21 June 1993, p.8.
66. Breese, K.S., One-price will stay, study says. *Automotive News*, 31 August 1992, p.1.
67. Rosamond, C. (1993) Lex will say yes to 'no haggle'. *Motor Dealer*, January.
68. Connelly, M. 'One-price' growth tapers off. *Automotive News*, 27 December 1993, p.28.
69. Robin, J.-C., interview, London, 1993.
70. Connelly, M., GM card far exceeds sales goal. *Automotive News*, 21 June 1993, pp.1, 43.
71. Sharfman, B. (1993) Carl Sewell. *Automobile*, July, p.70.
72. Costin, J.N., *Strategies for the Aftermarket – a Major Manufacturer's View*, the FT London Motor Conference, 17 February 1992.

73. Anonymous (1993) Great expectations. *Sewells International Car Digest*, **22**(3), 1.

74. *Financial Times*, 1 February 1992.

75. Uttal, B., Companies that serve you best. *Fortune*, 7 December 1987.

76. Freemantle, D. (1993) *Incredible Customer Service*, McGraw-Hill, London.

77. Keebler, J., NO SHO. *Automotive News Insight*, 17 May 1993, p.16i.

78. Jackson, K., Ford plans goodwill, roadside aid upgrades. *Automotive News*, 16 August 1993, p.4.

79. Seng, R.W. (1977) *The Skills of Selling*, AMACOM, New York.

80. Slingsby, H., If you run 400 branches or a tiny shop, don't forget who pays your wages. *Daily Telegraph*, London, 7 April 1993.

81. Burman, R. (1993) Customer-based engineering, design and serviceability examined. *Automotive Engineer*, February/March, p.47.

82. Bates, T., *Daily Telegraph*, London, 28 July 1993.

83. *Daily Telegraph*, 22 March 1994.

84. Frame, P., Saturn throws recall party. *Automotive News*, 16 August 1993, p.1.

85. Ogilvy & Mather AutoTrends Panel, 1990.

86. *Sunday Times*, 21 August 1994.

87. Woisetschläger, E., (1993) Kommentar. *Autohaus*, (23/24), 136.

88. Crain, K., Ford listens to dealers – and sells more cars. *Automotive News*, 4 April 1993, p.12.

89. Wade, P.V., *Relearning Customer Service at the US Auto Dealer*, ESOMAR Seminar, Paris, 11–13 November 1987.

90. Willman, J., Better service or your money back. *Financial Times*, 3 June 1993.

91. Anonymous (1993) Users blamed for breakdowns. *Company Car*, May, p.11. *Source: National Breakdown.*

92. Hazleton, L. (1993) *Confessions of a Fast Woman*, Flamingo, London.

93. Crain, K., The important thing. *Automotive News*, 14 June 1993, p.12.

94. Cutler, L., *Automotive News World Congress*, Detroit, 8 January 1990.

95. Sawyers, A., Twins carve separate sales niches in minivans. *Automotive News*, 26 April 1993, p.6.

96. Roddick, A., speech in November 1987.

97. Rehsche, M., Das Vertrauen der Kunden gewinnen. *Automobil Revue*, 14 October 1993, p.45.

98. Heslop, D., *The Management of Change*, transcription of a speech given in a private communication to the author.

99. Bayley, S. (1986) *Sex, Drink and Fast Cars – The Creation and Consumption of Images*, Faber and Faber, London.

100. Schwartzkopf, H.N. (1993) *It Doesn't Take a Hero*, Bantam Press, London.
101. MacDonald, B.G., GM takes new look at communication. *Automotive News*, 28 June 1993, p.14.
102. Power, C., Flops. *Business Week*, 16 August 1993.
103. Levitt, T. (1960) Marketing myopia. *Harvard Business Review*.
104. *Autohaus*, September 1994, p.20.
105. Lorenz, C., *Financial Times*, 3 June 1994.
106. Unisys (1993) *Customerize: A White Paper*.
107. Lorenz, C. (1986) *Notes From the Design Dimension – the New Competitive Weapon for Business*, Blackwell, Oxford.

Index